"Brad Jacobs shows how clear thinking and steady focus can turn big ideas into reality."
SUZANNE CLARK, President and CEO
U.S. Chamber of Commerce

"Brad delivers a book with a clear approach to creating billions and offers essential guidance on leading in a chaotic world."
MARK COSTA, Chairman and CEO
Eastman Chemical

"This book explains exactly how to build great companies from someone who has executed the playbook eight times."
DAVID COTE, former Chairman and CEO
Honeywell

"Brad's companies have delivered outstanding value for shareholders for decades. This book captures the principles behind that success."
WILL DANOFF, Fund Manager
Fidelity Contrafund

"Few entrepreneurs combine vision, execution, and integrity as masterfully as Brad Jacobs. His new book is a precise toolbox for those who refuse to mistake noise for success."
MATHIAS DÖPFNER, CEO
Axel Springer

"If you're someone who believes in thinking big, Brad's philosophy and strategies for growth in business and in life will surely resonate."
THASUNDA BROWN DUCKETT, President and CEO
TIAA

"Brad Jacobs has an impressive track record of building businesses, and in this book, he shares the key practices that underpin his success."
ROGER FERGUSON, former President and CEO
TIAA

"This expansive book delivers sharp insights that will empower you to raise your business to new heights."
LANCE FRITZ, former Chairman and CEO
Union Pacific Railroad

"An invaluable reminder that the best leaders combine humility, self-reflection, and clarity of purpose, empowering others to achieve greatness."
JOSH HARRIS, Founder
26North

"An engaging read from a serial value creator."
JAMIE IANNONE, President and CEO
eBay

"Few leaders have reshaped industries the way Brad has. His book is a rare combination of practical guidance and enduring inspiration."
MICHAEL KNEELAND, Chairman
United Rentals

"Brad's recipe, combining his personal habits with deep industry analysis, is an excellent roadmap for anyone wanting to create real value."
HENRY KRAVIS, Co-Founder and Co-Executive Chairman
KKR

"Brad Jacobs has mastered the art of creating value, and now his new book hands you the blueprint."
JORGE PAULO LEMANN, Chairman
Lemann Foundation

"Brad provides invaluable insight into his extraordinary success at the helm of multiple companies in the public markets."
LYNN MARTIN, President
New York Stock Exchange

"Brad Jacobs shows how lasting value is created through tenacity and strategic execution."
KEN MOELIS, Founder and Chairman
Moelis & Company

"Brad Jacobs's new book offers a whirlwind tour of how he thinks, plans, and works. Hold on to your seat."
MICHAEL MORITZ, Senior Advisor
Sequoia Heritage

"Brad stands at the top of the class in driving shareholder value. His books should be required reading at every business school."
JOHN O'LEARY, President and CEO
Daimler Truck North America

"Brad embraces challenges and turns them into opportunities. A great lesson in self-awareness and self-trust."
HEIDI PETZ, Chair, President and CEO
Sherwin-Williams

"Brad Jacobs is one of the most successful builders of enterprise value of our era. He does his homework and executes methodically. The results speak for themselves."
TED PICK, Chairman and CEO
Morgan Stanley

"Brad offers a fresh perspective on creating value that endures. A true game-changer."
ALEX RODRIGUEZ, Chairman and CEO
A-Rod Corp

"In his new book, Brad has succeeded in showing us, again, that he is a brilliant business genius."
RODOLPHE SAADÉ, Chairman
CMA CGM

"Brad's book shows how discipline, strategic clarity, and resilience build exceptional companies and leaders."
WAEL SAWAN, CEO
Shell

"This book captures the essence of what has made Brad a tremendously successful entrepreneur: a rigorous approach to business strategy combined with the emotional intelligence to lead organizations at scale."
MASAYOSHI SON, Founder, Chairman and CEO
SoftBank

"The only disappointment about this book is that I didn't have it in my hands 30 years ago. Brad provides rich insights for both business and life. Bravo!"
BOB SWAN, Operating Partner
Andreessen Horowitz

"Brad's remarkable track record of transforming companies makes this book indispensable."
JIM UMPLEBY, Executive Chairman
Caterpillar

"Brad Jacobs has a gift for turning ordinary businesses into something golden, time and time again."
BARBARA VAN ALLEN, President and CEO
The Economic Club of New York

"A compelling read for anyone aspiring to build something monumental."
ROBIN VINCE, Chairman and CEO
BNY

"A profound guide that unites lessons on corporate integration and the spiritual self while urging us to harness new technology for a more prosperous society."
DAME EMMA WALMSLEY, CEO
GSK

"It's inspiring to me that one of our nation's most successful business leaders is sharing his hands-on approach to building iconic companies."
ED WOLFE, Founder and CEO
Wolfe Research

"Brad's distinctive insights stand out as both powerful and truly inspiring."
ERIC YUAN, Founder and CEO
Zoom

How to Make a Few *More* Billion Dollars

How to Make a Few More Billion Dollars

BRAD JACOBS

GREENLEAF
BOOK GROUP PRESS

As a reminder to my readers (and current and future investors), past performance does not guarantee future results, and my future ventures might or might not be as fruitful for investors as my previous ones. Nothing I say in this book should be construed as a promise regarding future performance.

Published by Greenleaf Book Group Press

Austin, Texas
www.gbgpress.com

Distributed by Greenleaf Book Group

For ordering information or special discounts for bulk purchases, please contact Greenleaf Book Group at PO Box 91869, Austin, TX 78709, 512.891.6100.

Design and composition by Greenleaf Book Group and Mimi Bark

Publisher's Cataloging-in-Publication data is available.

Print ISBN: 979-8-88645-465-9

eBook ISBN: 979-8-88645-466-6

To offset the number of trees consumed in the printing of our books, Greenleaf donates a portion of the proceeds from each printing to the Arbor Day Foundation. Greenleaf Book Group has replaced over 50,000 trees since 2007.

Printed in the United States of America on acid-free paper

25 26 27 28 29 30 31 32   13 12 11 10 9 8 7 6 5 4 3 2 1

First Edition

To Fred Smith—visionary, lionheart, and friend.
Your ideas changed industries, but your
kindness changed lives, including mine.

Contents

Acknowledgments xv

Introduction 1

Chapter 1: Finding Your Center—Meditation
and Mental Synthesis 7

Chapter 2: Making Your Way Back to Center 29

Chapter 3: Choosing the Right Industry to Consolidate 57

Chapter 4: Raising Tons of Money 73

Chapter 5: Mastering the Integration Playbook 93

Chapter 6: Organizational Integration 109

Chapter 7: Tech Integration 129

Conclusion: The Ultimate Opportunity 155

Appendix 1: Summary of Book One: *How to Make
a Few Billion Dollars* (2023) 179

Appendix 2: Timeline of Unnatural Selection 225

Appendix 3: Humanity's 13.8-Billion-Year Profit
and Loss Statement 233

Appendix 4: Thought Experiments 237

Appendix 5: Sources of Equity Capital 245

Sources and Further Reading 259

Notes 263

Index 265

About the Author 279

Acknowledgments

AS ALWAYS, MY DEEPEST gratitude goes to my wife, Lamia. You've supported me on every level, and for more than 40 years, you've been my greatest source of motivation and strength.

My heartfelt thanks to Lucy Peterson for the gift of perspective and for grounding my wildest ideas.

Thank you to Jack DiGiovanni, Michael Haidet, David Ragan, and Noelia Valero for keeping me on track.

And to Greenleaf Book Group—I recognize this is the fastest book you've ever published, and your speed inspires me.

Finally, to the QXO executive leadership team, thank you for letting me bounce ideas off you and for breathing life into my boldest notions.

Introduction

I PUBLISHED MY FIRST BOOK, *How to Make a Few Billion Dollars*, in 2023, and at the time, I had no idea it would become a bestseller. I wrote it to reflect on how the companies I've led have created tens of billions of dollars in stock appreciation and to share those reflections with anyone who wants to achieve big things. I was surprised by how deeply this resonated with people, especially when I discussed mistakes I've made. Some parts captivated readers; others didn't quite land. But, importantly to me, I started getting inquiries from people on topics I didn't cover enough—or at all. These are the questions I've received most frequently in one form or another:

- How do you stay calm amid chaos?

- What kinds of meditation do you do?

- If you're rattled, how do you get back to your center?

- Are some industry attributes more essential than others when it comes to building a billion-dollar enterprise through consolidation?

- What types of industries should be avoided, even if they seem promising?

- How exactly do you raise the billions of dollars needed to fund your vision?

- What are the pros and cons of each type of investor?

- How do you integrate a company after you buy it?

- What are the most important things you do to increase the profitability of a company you buy?

- How do you build a culture that people are excited to join and proud to stay with for years?

- What responsibilities do entrepreneurs and technologists have in shaping the future of artificial intelligence (AI)?

- How do you think AI will impact the future of business and humanity?

This sequel provides those answers. For those who haven't

read my first book or would like a quick refresher, I've included a summary of key takeaways in Appendix 1.

I'd like to make one thing clear right off the bat: I'm no mythical figure with a Midas touch. Those are just sensational headlines. My special talent—my superpower, if you will—is much simpler: Birds fly. Fish swim. I start companies from scratch, assemble teams capable of extraordinary success, and turn abstract ideas into billions of dollars of tangible value. But I'm far from perfect. Psychologist Albert Ellis nailed it when he said, "We're all fallible, fucked-up human beings." Well, count me among them.

When I create a company, it starts in my mind. I want to have a very clear mental picture of what the business will look like out of the gate, then a year later, five years later, a decade later. Next, I gather a group of supersmart people to be the founding management team. Having great leadership talent on board is a huge milestone. I tell them, "Here's my vision" and challenge everyone to poke holes in the plan and suggest ways to improve it. I listen carefully and gather lots of perspectives; then I retreat into solitude to reflect, visualize, and strategize. It's in these quiet moments that I make my best decisions. The picture of what we're planning to do is so vivid that, for the most part, the hardest work is over before the implementation begins.

There's something magical about conceiving a monumental idea and then—hot damn!—seeing it actually materialize over a few years. It's a profoundly creative process. For me, creating shareholder value isn't just financial; it's about bringing something extraordinary into existence from absolutely nothing. Imagine this: One moment, you've got an idea, and before you know it, you're looking at 150,000 employees, billions in profit, and a soaring stock price on the New York Stock Exchange. It's the ultimate feat of business alchemy.

Here's the crucial thing: You've got to think extraordinarily big from day one. Nobody achieves massive success by thinking small and hoping to become big. And sure, not everyone can or wants to make a few billion dollars, let alone a few *more* billion dollars, but everyone can learn to think more creatively. Whether your ambition is to consolidate an industry or become an outstanding parent, an Olympic athlete, or a celebrated artist, a proper mindset is essential. The ability to rearrange your brain and create that mindset is entirely within your grasp.

If you do want to make a lot of money, you have to move fast. Be decisive, confident, courageous. You're not going to make all the right moves. Chances are, you'll make some dumb decisions—maybe a few dozen swings and misses out of thousands of decisions over time. As long as they aren't fatal mistakes that derail the whole business plan, you can afford a misstep here and there. And yes, taking appropriate risks is part of the gig. If you won't accept some risk, you won't achieve much.

To me, it feels like one of those hospital dramas on TV, where nonstop crises need immediate resolution. There's always something urgent happening, like tech rolling out faster than HR can hire technologists or an explosion in capital requirements. I'm constantly on the hunt for opportunities with a high probability of success—a massive upside and a manageable downside. I have major shareholders who have put their money where their trust is—in me and my team—as well as a number of friends, neighbors, and relatives who have gone all in. It's a lot of weight to carry, but I thrive in this environment. And I channel the pressure into a relentless drive.

And always, you've got to love what you do. I love being a CEO. I get up early and work seven days a week. If there were eight days in a week, I'd happily work another day. It's a blast. I love the people, the challenges, and the electricity of having a winning team around me. Every day feels like a day off because I'm doing what I enjoy alongside colleagues I trust and respect. To be able to create tens of billions of dollars of value for shareholders—that's cool stuff. Seven multibillion-dollar companies later, I can say, unequivocally, that it's been a thrill every time.

My first book walked through each company I founded, and I remember the pride I felt as I was writing all that down. It drove home the fact that my businesses have delivered amazing returns on inaugural share prices, including a 50x return on XPO stock and a 200x return on United Rentals stock. It's gratifying to be the architect of that much value.

A lot of it comes down to striving for clarity and reducing my own bias. I can look at a situation and know where I went wrong and where I got it right. I can see the idiosyncrasies—even the eccentricities—that enable my team's success. And I'm comfortable with a little bit of anxiety, even fear, when facing a decision that has huge consequences because I believe that's a healthy trait in a leader. I covered these concepts in book one, and I've included a lot more detail here in the first two chapters.

If you're someone who believes in thinking big but is not sure where to start, I hope this book opens that door for you. Ants haul up to 50 times their weight. Starfish regrow lost limbs. I build multibillion-dollar companies. And maybe, just maybe, you can create your own billion-dollar legacy too.

CHAPTER 1

Finding Your Center— Meditation and Mental Synthesis

A human being is part of a whole, called by us "universe"—a part limited in time and space. He experiences himself, his thoughts and feelings, as something separated from the rest. . . . Our task must be to free ourselves from this prison by widening our circle of compassion . . .

—**Albert Einstein, on the optical delusion of consciousness**

IN BUSINESS, AS IN LIFE, achieving goals on a grand scale isn't merely a function of strategy or hard work, although these are undeniably important. Mental clarity is even more vital to your success. Throughout my 46 years as a CEO and entrepreneur, I've discovered that maintaining a clear, balanced mindset is essential to strong leadership, not just for good decision-making or resilience in the face of challenges, but also because clarity gives you a huge edge. Whether your big goal involves launching a start-up or steering a multibillion-dollar enterprise, how you manage your inner state can be the determining factor. It's imperative to center your mind.

> **Keeping your head in a good place is crucial for business success.**

Inner Control and Success

Centering has been a recurring theme in my life since I was 14 years old. My first meaningful exposure to centering came at a summer enrichment camp at Northfield Mount Hermon School in Massachusetts. Our philosophy instructor handed out a book called *Centering in Pottery, Poetry, and the Person* by M. C. Richards. I vividly remember the cover: a pair of hands balancing a clay vase between open palms. The message resonated deeply with me: Before creating anything of value, I first needed to get myself centered. This idea has guided me ever since.

Another book we read that summer was *Tao Te Ching*, by the Chinese philosopher Lao Tzu. It speaks to the concepts of inner stillness, balance, and aligning with the natural flow of life. Two of Lao Tzu's most powerful tenets are "Knowing others is intelligence; knowing yourself is true wisdom" and "Mastering others is strength; mastering yourself is true power."[1] From the sixth century BC to today, the philosophy behind those words holds true: Our success flows from inner control.

> **Arrogance is the enemy in both business and life.**

As I described in my earlier book, I'm an advocate of what I call *rearranging the brain*—consciously reshaping thought patterns, perceptions, and emotions to access more expansive ways of being. I don't believe there's ever a point when a person has fully broadened their perspective in life, with nothing more to do. I've never met anyone who is so enlightened they're in a state of Nirvana. Just as Lean Six Sigma is the model for continuous improvement in the business world, mind transformation techniques take continuous practice— a genuine heart-and-soul commitment to break free of the "optical delusion of consciousness" Einstein warned against.

After *How to Make a Few Billion Dollars* came out, I heard from many people who loved the meditation and rearranging-your-brain stuff but wanted me to share exactly what I do when I meditate. I've dedicated this first chapter to detailing my personal meditation practices. To be clear, I'm not a meditation teacher or a guru; I'm a fellow explorer who meditates twice a day, every day, to chill out and stay centered. My goal is to share what works for me so you can discover what works best for you.

Mental Synthesis

Before we explore meditation techniques, it's important to understand the underlying mechanism of imagination— what cognitive scientists refer to as *mental synthesis*. This is the brain's ability to create new scenarios by combining elements from memory. It enables us to visualize possibilities, connect unrelated ideas, and direct our focus toward the outcomes we desire.

Roughly a million years ago, early *Homo erectus* began

gathering in the evenings around fire, which scientists posit may have driven a shift in cognitive capabilities. Prior to this, human thought processes were probably rooted in the immediate present, with little capacity for reflection. Over time, as the human brain evolved, *Homo erectus* developed a rudimentary ability to merge distinct memories into new mental images, marking the beginning of human creativity and forward thinking. Without this evolutionary leap, there would be no abstract thought and no complex ability to problem-solve in business or in life.

> **Mental synthesis is how we imagine**
> **what doesn't exist. Then we build it.**

Today, it's impossible to imagine navigating a day without the benefit of mental synthesis. Life is full of decisions about future necessities. The visualization techniques I use to center myself—from picturing the universe to feeling love—are all practical applications of this innate capability for abstract thought we humans take for granted. The balance of this chapter will explore how mental synthesis can empower you to find your own center by trying different meditation techniques.

My Own Meditation Path

I began transcendental meditation (TM) when I was 16 years old. I happened to see a poster of Maharishi Mahesh Yogi that said something like "Life Is Bliss," and I thought, *Bliss? I'll take some of that.* The poster was advertising a free introductory lecture on TM, and Maharishi had this intriguing look—long hair, a wise, peaceful face—like someone who had figured out a secret that the rest of us were missing. I figured, *Why not?* Off I went, and liking what I heard, I started practicing meditation twice a day. I've been doing that for decades, without missing a single day. You could say a poster changed my life.

> Meditation is a tool for sharper decisions
> and bolder visions, not just relaxation.

TM is a process of thinking a thought in an increasingly abstract way, until you go beyond the thought and experience a state of unbounded awareness. One metaphor that's sometimes used is the ocean, where all evident activity is near the surface—waves, fish, boats, birds—and the more you sink down into the depths, the more boundless and abstract it becomes. In those early days, meditation felt to me like entering a vast space that was both calming and exhilarating at the same time. I was hooked. It wasn't just about the relaxation; I was discovering a deeper, subtler state of awareness that was beyond everyday thought yet profoundly practical for daily life. Maharishi had described it as experiencing bliss within yourself, and for me, it delivered exactly that: a sense of ease that made everything feel more manageable.

After years of practicing meditation, I traveled to Switzerland and India to study with Maharishi himself. He barely slept and had this habit of meeting people at bizarre hours, like four or five o'clock in the morning. The rest of the time, he was meditating or teaching. During one of our conversations, I confessed that I'd modified some advanced techniques— doing things my own way, finding bliss in ways that weren't strictly by the book. For example, with one meditation technique, instead of directing my attention to my solar plexus, I was placing it at the middle of my forehead because that felt more natural and blissful to me. Maharishi just laughed. "We're doing research into consciousness as a field of all possibilities," he told me. "If it's natural and blissful, Brad, go for it." Those words freed me to explore even more deeply, blending meditation with other schools of thought, including Milton H. Erickson's self-hypnosis, Richard Bandler's

Neuro-Linguistic Programming, Paramahansa Yogananda's Kriya Yoga, and the teachings of Thích Nhất Hạnh, the father of mindfulness.

My Morning Non-Routine Routine

As you can probably guess, my morning routine is not predictable at all. I don't want to do the same thing every time. By the time this book is published, no doubt my "routine" will have evolved from what I'm describing here, and to my mind, that's ideal. Meditation for me is not about replicating a particular experience; it's about profoundly letting go. And it's not a mechanical process; it's just the opposite: freeing my mind from all active modalities and settling into pure quietness.

There are some steps I go through to prepare for meditation—again, nothing rigid or prescribed. I go with what feels natural to me in the moment. These days, I typically start with yoga. The yoga poses don't take long, maybe six or seven minutes in total. I hold each position for 10 to 30 seconds and emphasize the positions where my head is lower than my waist so blood flows to my brain.

Then, I often do some Qigong techniques, which combine breathing with posture and the visualization of time, space, feelings, or thoughts. This utilizes many different parts of the brain. One Qigong exercise I especially enjoy is called *raising the qi* (the life force). I slowly, deeply inhale and exhale while holding my hands in front of my navel and moving them upward while I'm inhaling and downward while I'm exhaling. I move them up a little higher with each new inhalation. This is calming, and at the same time, it improves posture and mind–body connection. Raising the qi gives me a warm feeling of being immersed in all the love in the entirety of existence, putting me into a blissful frame of mind to start the day.

While Qigong-inspired visualizations expand consciousness outward, I also want to turn my focus inward before I meditate. For this, I use techniques I adapted from hypnotherapy to deepen the connection between my mind and body. I'll do a technique, based on a Qigong practice, where I open my hands outward, close my eyes, and think, *I am* in *the universe.* As I do this, I'm picturing the entire observable universe—all 546,000 billion trillion miles of it. I let myself become a mind without a body, floating in a vast, mostly empty space. It's a very liberating feeling.

Then I'll bring my arms inward, cupping them as if I'm holding a globe or egg in front of me, and think, *And the universe is in* me. I picture Hiranyagarbha, the Hindu golden egg of the universe, between my hands. I lift that imaginary egg to my mouth and, visualizing the universe being placed in my mouth, I swallow it, repeating silently, *The universe is in* me.

Sometimes I'll take it further. After I swallow the universe, I'll think, *I* love *the universe* and feel love pouring out of me, filling every speck of the cosmos. Then I'll think, *And the universe loves* me, as my arms come in, almost like a self-hug. I imagine this is how a baby might feel wrapped in a mother's hug but multiplied by a million. If I want to deepen the experience, I envision not just the universe but the multiverse—an infinite number of universes spreading out in every possible direction. *I'm* in *the multiverse. And the multiverse is in* me. I can sense my love radiating outward to every corner of the multiverse and feel its love streaming into me. It's a wonderful way to start the morning—inebriating in the best way.

I'll do variations of my universe and multiverse visualization techniques, always ending with being immersed in all the love in the cosmos. It puts me into a completely different state of awareness—one that helps me enter a blissful frame of mind. It also stimulates creativity. And it reminds me of the gigantic context that informs all our lives, which helps keep things in perspective in business. When the inevitable problems of the day hit, they seem small by comparison.

The next step in my non-routine routine is something I learned when I studied under a brilliant hypnotherapist named Ernie Rossi. I would visit Ernie and his wife at their home in California for three days at a time, once or twice a year. This went on for a few years. During most of those visits, Ernie put me into a guided hypnotic trance state that's so radically different from being awake that it's hard to describe. The best way I can put it is a kind of blend between dreaming, fantasizing, watching a brightly colored cartoon, remembering long-forgotten memories, and reliving things that took place a long, long time ago. At the same time, it felt contemporaneous, not in the past. I was discovering all kinds of new interactions between the senses—smelling sights, hearing tastes, and touching emotions, for example— and visualizing future potentialities. Instead of the nice, neat bifurcations that define so much of our waking existence, the lines were blurred.

One classic exercise Ernie developed was the mind–hand connection. I've used my own modification of this with my management teams for years. The idea is that if you stare at your hands long enough, it stimulates the brain. It's believed that this "hidden" mind–hand connection stems from our evolution from primates, when superior manual dexterity aligned with the development of neuro-wiring in the motor cortex region of the brain. It's recognized across cultures as well; if you go to a mosque, you'll see worshippers raise their hands and gaze at their palms while praying. This has a deep emotional and spiritual resonance for a lot of Muslims.

Try it now: Stare at your hands as if you've never seen them before. This puts most people into a unique state of mental relaxation, creativity, and focus. You might see colors or creases in your hands you've never noticed before. When I use the technique myself, I stare at my hands as I inhale, and I picture my breath coming in through my right hand. When I breathe out, my breath is passing through my left hand. I don't need to do this for long to get into an unbounded state of awareness—maybe four or five breaths in and out. It's both calming and energizing. And I never know what will emerge as I breathe through my palms. Sometimes it's the universe, multiverse, or all the love they contain. Sometimes I'm breathing in the image of someone I love through my right hand and breathing out something toxic through my left hand.

This is often the moment when gratitude kicks in. I breathe in things I'm grateful for in my life through my right hand and breathe out negativity through the left. Then I sit without back support, with my spine very straight, as if there's a string pulling my head up to the ceiling, and do what's called pranayama, an Indian form of breath control. *Prana* is the Sanskrit counterpart to the Chinese word *qi*. As I do several minutes of slow, deep breathing, I'm picturing warmth, light, and energy coming in through the base of my spine, up my spinal cord, and out the top of my head.

This may sound like a lot of techniques, but my pre-meditation exercises typically take only 20 minutes total, sometimes less, before I begin meditating. You can experiment and settle on a few techniques that work best for you, or do your own adaptations. Because I've practiced so many different meditation styles in my life, I never know in advance what experience I'm in for, so I go into each session open, receptive, and curious about what movie will play in the private cinema of my mind.

Numinous Experiences

In 1917, German philosopher Rudolf Otto coined the term *numinosum*, which he described as a fusion of awe, mystery, and novelty.[2] It might be a moment of spiritual ecstasy, or the sense of a supernatural presence, or a profound connection to the transcendent—like being transfixed by nature or art. In short, a numinous experience is one that is new, is inspiring, and makes goose bumps tingle on your skin. Moments like witnessing a child's first genuine smile, feeling the cool mist from a towering waterfall, or holding your spouse's hand on a quiet walk are numinous for many people.

> **Your best ideas won't come from thinking harder, but from thinking in different ways.**

Each of us can actively create numinous experiences. Breathing in and out isn't inherently numinous, but breathing love into the universe can be. A musical chord alone is not numinous, but an inspiring series of notes and chords can be. I want to become that music and live a life filled with numinous experiences. Numinosity is a high priority for me as a person, an entrepreneur, and a CEO because it enhances the creativity that inspires success. Meditation is my main method for achieving that.

Playing with Time, Space, and Love

A lot of what I do with meditation these days has to do with changing perspectives, such as looking at space from a different perspective than the way we humans think about space from our little piece of Earth, or even through the lens of NASA's most powerful eye, the James Webb Space Telescope. I use meditation to expand my mind from the Earth to our Sun, through the Solar System, across the Galaxy, and outward through the universe and beyond—visualizing my mind with no body, floating in cosmic space.

You can play with this technique in all kinds of ways during meditation. For example, I may expand my awareness like an accordion, stretching across galaxies, bathing in the exhilarating multiverse, then contracting to compress into subatomic space. I'll visualize going inside a molecule, then into an atom, into its nucleus, and finally, deep inside, to the gluons, the force carriers. I'll do the same thing with time, picturing my life over the last few decades, then going back centuries and millennia. I'll keep going back 13.8 billion years to the Big Bang, sometimes earlier. And I can switch it up again, coming all the way forward, picturing the world going on and on into the future.

Different things work for different people, but these experiments in repositioning time and space give me context. They remind me to be humble, that I'm just one small part of something much more profound, and a tiny part at that. At the same time, I'm part of a big time-and-space contraption I share with every other person and thing, animate and inanimate. The juxtaposition of these two perspectives gives me a deeper understanding.

My Meditation Movie Screen

The meditation exercises I just described are thought experiments, and, yes, they create some control over the experience. But more often, I practice mindful meditation, which is like watching a movie. I'm not the director, the producer, or even an actor; I'm simply the audience, sitting with my proverbial bag of popcorn, attentively observing whatever unfolds on the screen of my mind. And because mindful meditation is the softest, gentlest state of receptivity, anything can happen in that movie. I don't resist it. I've prepared my mind to be superfluid beyond the boundaries of time and space.

I might experience pure nothingness, like looking up at a night sky with no stars. Absolute blackness. Or it can be the opposite—a phantasmagoria of thousands or even millions of colors and lights, some of which I've never seen in real life. They exist only in my meditation mind's eye. My meditation movie might show me geometric patterns with billions of extraordinary details, with a logic that makes perfect sense.

But it would make no sense whatsoever if I were to open my eyes and try to explain it to somebody else. How could I explain something that's unbounded by time and space?

Sometimes my mind's eye sees favorite places or moments imbued with happiness from years ago, like the love of my mother. If the experience is strong enough, I may break my rule of being simply receptive and jump into the movie to amplify the experience. This is something I learned from Richard Bandler's teachings on Neuro-Linguistic Programming. If I'm feeling loving vibrations, I can say to myself, *I now magnify the feeling tenfold, then a hundredfold* and—boom!—that will happen.

More often, though, I remain a mindful observer of the movie simply by being in tune with any perceptions that emerge. If my breath gets attached to sensory or emotional perceptions, I can breathe those in and digest them. Or, if it's more of an integration between mind and body, my awareness may start at the bottom of my spine and then travel to my solar plexus—or my heart, throat, lips, nostrils, eyeballs, the space between my eyebrows, the middle of my forehead. Each mind–body connection will elicit a different experience.

Once you become adept at being receptive to vibrations, it's easy to apply this to your life. Here's a technique I learned from John and Julie Gottman, the psychologists and relationship experts. Scientists have found that a 20-second hug can generate oxytocin, the so-called love hormone.[3] So I picture hugging someone in my family, often my wife or my mom, and holding that hug for 20 seconds or more. This creates love vibes that I can magnify a hundredfold, then infinitely, until my entire consciousness is saturated with love.

> **In high-stakes business situations, emotional balance is a powerful advantage.**

Importantly, meditation in all its forms is more than just a concept. It helps keep you in the zone with your head in a good place and gives you the skills to think differently while maintaining an inner peace. Consider the techniques I described in terms of the benefits they deliver: humility, positivity, the headspace to think expansively, relaxation and rejuvenation amid chaos, the ability to keep problems in context, boundless creativity, and the capacity to be inspired. These are essential qualities for anyone who wants to achieve a phenomenal goal.

Feeling the Brain

I stumbled on my feeling the brain technique after one of my hypnosis sessions with Ernie Rossi, inspired by his mind–hand exercise I described earlier. Instead of staring at my right and left hands, I decided to "stare" at the right and left hemispheres of my brain. My awareness might float into the right part of my brain or the left part. Sometimes I allow it to float back and forth between the two. At other times, the experience seems to have a mind of its own, and my awareness settles in another part of my brain altogether—for example, the precise center of my brain.

If you put a string from the right half of my brain to the left, from the top to the bottom, and from the front to the back, the point where those three strings intersect is a special meditation spot for me. I discovered this by visualizing that exact spot and allowing my consciousness to experience it. This triggered intense creativity, as well as all kinds of positive sensory and emotional experiences. But ecstatic experiences occur most often when I allow my awareness to float in the top of my head, eliciting a whole new level of phantasmagoric display.

As much as I love that sensation, I find it valuable to spend most of my meditation time with awareness in all parts of my brain at once. I simply "feel" my entire brain inside my skull, sitting on top of the trillions of cells and atoms that make up my body. The unique consciousness and sheer humanness of my being make me part of something fantastically huge, mysterious, and important. This is exciting to contemplate, and it can trigger all kinds of experiences.

> **Every great company starts as an audacious idea that someone dared to take seriously.**

Feeling the brain is also a great on-the-go technique. If I'm off-center for whatever reason during the day, I close my eyes and sense awareness flowing through my brain. For me, it's as if an imaginary electrical cord from my spine, brain, and body gets plugged into a high-voltage outlet—immediate rejuvenation. After I introduced feeling the brain in my first book, it's been gratifying to hear from readers who are creating their own experiences using the practice.

Toward Your Own Center

I hope this chapter has given you a taste of various ways you can explore meditation. You'll discover what works for you given your own personality, physiology, psychology, and life experiences.

The techniques I describe, from expanding into the multiverse to feeling the quiet awareness within your own brain, are all paths to the same destination: your center. This is where you'll find the mental clarity and resilience necessary for success in any field. In the next chapter, I'll discuss some powerful psychological frameworks you can use to return to your center when life throws you off-balance.

CHAPTER 2

Making Your Way Back to Center

IN THE PRIOR CHAPTER, I shared the various meditation practices I use to get into the zone, a place of deep peace and effortless receptivity. Now, I'll talk about how I get back to the zone and return to my center when I lose touch with it.

Even though I've been practicing meditation for more than half a century, I still get kicked out of the zone from time to time. These days, it happens much less frequently than it used to when I was younger, and I can recenter more quickly. But I still find myself outside the zone looking in sometimes, and so will you. When that happens, I use one or more of the five techniques in my return-to-center tool-box. They are Albert Ellis's rational emotive behavior therapy (REBT), Aaron Beck's cognitive behavioral therapy (CBT), Marsha Linehan's dialectical behavior therapy (DBT), Martin Seligman's positive psychology, and mindfulness. I'm going to focus specifically on recentering, although all five of these approaches have broad applications as tools for mental and emotional well-being. Perhaps some will work for you—or maybe they'll inspire you to find your own ways to recenter, ways I never even thought of.

In any endeavor, it's important to keep the ups and downs in perspective, especially the downs. Losing your center is not a failure, and perfection is both impossible and undesirable. To fully grasp this, consider how the universe and our own human traits evolved, before we dig into the toolbox.

An Imperfect 13.8 Billion Years

The history of the cosmos is filled with chaos, imbalances, and extinction events—things that went bump in the night, again and again. But those bumps didn't break the universe; they built it. Thirteen billion years ago, matter and antimatter, in theory, should have canceled each other out. Instead, from the tiniest imbalance—just a sliver more matter than antimatter—the scaffolding of the universe was born. It was disruption, not harmony, that fueled the creation of matter and evolution.

Nearly everything we know or infer about the development of the universe after the Big Bang points to asymmetry, anomaly, and error. Atoms needed instability to bond into molecules, which needed asymmetry to give rise to life. And life, through countless random mutations, gave rise to human brains that now ponder the imperfections that made them possible. The rest is a stunning history of beautiful mistakes. If perfection had ever ruled at any point, you and I likely wouldn't be here.

> Success comes from persistence and the ability to act quickly, rather than from aiming for perfection.

I know that our brilliantly flawed universe will inevitably generate some outcomes I don't like. Not only am I okay with that, I also recognize that good things can come from those outcomes, or at the very least, I can learn from them. When I stopped expecting flawlessness from myself and others, I could let go of frustration and put that energy to good use.

I believe in this imperfection mindset so strongly that I've woven it into the culture of each new company I start. Mistakes aren't failures; they're the very substance of growth.

The next section provides some context on why driven people often try to control every variable to perfection. Here again, once you understand the origin, it can help you stay constructive in the present.

How Human Traits Evolved

Getting back to center requires understanding what knocked you out of the zone in the first place. It's helpful to know the broader reasons why the modern human mind shows certain maladaptive traits, which are often directed inward at ourselves.

Darwin's theory of evolution explains how gradual adaptations to the environment, accumulated over vast stretches of time, give rise to new species. Traits that improve survival and reproduction become more common, shaping the course of life. This same process eventually produced our species, *Homo sapiens*. Yet because evolution unfolds at such a slow pace, we still carry traits that were once adaptive but now create friction in modern life.

Take the fight-or-flight response. For our more skittish ancestors, catastrophizing harmless rustles in the bushes gave them a survival edge over those who ignored potential threats. Their vigilance was passed down. Today, that same wiring can leave us anxious in safe environments. We pump adrenaline, our hearts race, we sweat. Prolonged, it can sap energy, heighten tension, and leave us caught in cycles of worry.

Understanding the evolutionary roots of these feelings can restore clarity. Anxiety and pessimism, once vital to avoiding danger, now often manifest as excessive risk avoidance. As a serial CEO, I couldn't have built global public companies without embracing calculated risk. Seeing obstructive feelings through the lens of evolution reminds me that these feelings are echoes of the past, not accurate guides for contemporary decisions.

The same is true of our tendency toward perfectionism and self-criticism. In early human history, an intense focus on doing things exactly right could mean the difference between life and death. Venturing carelessly outside a cave might expose someone to predators while extreme caution—whether in hunting or weathering storms—helped ensure survival and the passing on of genes. Today, though, that perfectionist streak can make us harsh with ourselves and others, even when there are no life-or-death stakes.

When we recognize these inherited tendencies for what they are—outdated survival strategies—we give ourselves the power to step out of their grip. Evolution explains why anxiety and self-criticism show up so strongly, but it doesn't dictate how we respond to external events today.

Rational Emotive Behavior Therapy (REBT)

A note up front: The lion's share of the toolbox content is split between REBT and CBT because those sections contain useful lists of things to try yourself. This could make them feel more important. However, I consider dialectical behavior therapy, positive psychology, and mindfulness to be equally useful tools for getting back into the zone and recentering. All five approaches have worked reliably well for me over the years.

> It's inevitable that you'll get knocked off-center.
> What matters is finding your way back.

Albert Ellis and REBT is a natural place to start. Ellis was one of the great psychotherapists of the 20th century, right up there with Sigmund Freud, Carl Jung, and Aaron Beck. I first met him in a group setting at one of his famous Friday teach-ins at the Albert Ellis Institute in Manhattan. The highlight of those evenings was when he would call for volunteers from the audience and sit them down one-on-one in front of the group, then ask them to name something that was deeply troubling to them. People would share something that was making them angry, anxious, or depressed—clearly taking them out of their peaceful zone.

Ellis would then ask the person to close their eyes and get in tune with that negative emotion. When he felt they were ready, he'd say "Okay, now make yourself half as upset as you just were." He'd let them sit in silence for a minute or two and then ask, "Do you now feel roughly half as upset?" If the person said yes, he'd respond, "Okay, great. Now open your eyes," followed by "Tell me what you told yourself in order to feel less upset by half." The person would answer something like, "My boss is acting like a jerk, but so what? He's under a lot of pressure, and I'm optimistic that once that passes, he'll return to his pleasant self" or "Sure, I have an illness I wish I didn't have, but it's not fatal. I can live with it." This was a brilliantly simple technique because Ellis was demonstrating that external events, in and of themselves, don't make you upset; what makes you upset is what you tell yourself.

In my experience, most people carry on an intermittent internal monologue of self-criticism. It's a quiet, often unspoken commentary—invasive, persistent, and deeply personal. We rarely voice it aloud, not because it isn't there, but because we're afraid of being vulnerable or appearing weak if we show our imperfections. The paradox in that thinking is that none of us are perfect, yet each of us thinks we're inadequate. In fact, nearly everyone I know underestimates their own worth.

> ## Successful people are humble. They know they're not always right.

Often, people who appear outwardly confident—even arrogant—are actually masking internal self-doubt. Scratch the surface, and you'll rarely find someone who genuinely believes in their own perfection. Maybe they dislike their appearance, their background, or some other imagined shortcoming. It's what Ellis referred to as *stinkin' thinkin'*. If your failure to be perfect is what's throwing you off-center, you're certainly not alone. And I was right there with you at one time.

Ellis's work profoundly reshaped my understanding of perfectionism. I used to hold myself to punishingly high standards, demanding constant excellence and leaving no margin for error. Unsurprisingly, this only led to disappointment. Ellis taught me to reframe rigid demands as flexible preferences—to aim high but not crumble if I fell short. By embracing the inevitability of human error, I discovered a more resilient mindset and a far healthier foundation for both my business endeavors and my personal relationships.

Through his REBT, Ellis helped millions of people confront and reshape their irrational, self-defeating beliefs. In his books, he describes stinkin' thinkin' as a psychological imbalance rooted in the harmful self-talk people often engage in—unfair expectations and irrational self-criticism. The core of his therapy is to identify those beliefs and reframe them into more rational ones.

> To think constructively, learn to recognize your irrational beliefs and cognitive distortions and how to reframe them.

Rather than interpret what I learned from Ellis, I'll share these three quotes from his book *How to Stubbornly Refuse to Make Yourself Miserable About Anything—Yes, Anything!*[1]

"No matter how badly you act, no matter how unfairly others treat you, no matter how crummy the conditions you live under are—you virtually always have the ability and the power to change your intense feelings of anxiety, despair, and hostility. Not only can you decrease them; you can annihilate and remove them."

"When you rigidly hold certain irrational beliefs—when you dogmatically command that you must do well, have to be approved by others, have got to have people treat you fairly, and always ought to live with easy and enjoyable conditions—when you stoutly hold these irrational beliefs, you will tend to make yourself needlessly miserable and will probably defeat some of your most cherished goals."

"You largely (not completely) create and control your own disturbed thoughts and feelings, and therefore you have the power to radically change them."

Below are 18 examples of commonly held irrational beliefs. It's an ugly list. You might recognize some of them as beliefs you hold. Or you might see some mirrored in a friend or work colleague. Each irrational belief is followed by a reframed, more constructive, rational belief designed to improve your mindset.

1. **Irrational belief:** I must be liked by everyone to feel good about myself.

   Rational belief: I prefer to be liked, but I can still value myself, even if some people don't like me.

2. **Irrational belief:** If I make a mistake, it means I'm a failure.

   Rational belief: Everyone makes mistakes. They're part of learning and don't define my worth.

3. **Irrational belief:** Bad things shouldn't happen to me.

   Rational belief: Life is unpredictable. Bad things happen to everyone. It's how I deal with them that matters.

4. **Irrational belief:** I must be perfect, or I am worthless.

   Rational belief: Perfection is unrealistic—no one is perfect, but I still have value as a person, even with my flaws.

5. **Irrational belief:** If people criticize me, it proves there's something inherently wrong with me.

   Rational belief: Criticism is about behavior, not my worth as a person. I can learn from it without losing self-esteem.

6. **Irrational belief:** People must always agree with me. If they don't, they're being difficult.

   Rational belief: Others are entitled to their own perspectives; disagreement doesn't mean disrespect.

7. **Irrational belief:** Others must treat me fairly, or they are awful people.

   Rational belief: It's preferable when others treat me fairly, but I can't control their behavior—only my response.

8. **Irrational belief:** I can't be happy unless everything is exactly how I want it.

   Rational belief: I can find contentment even when circumstances aren't ideal.

9. **Irrational belief:** I must be in control of everything, or I'll fall apart.

Rational belief: I can handle uncertainty. Control is helpful but not always necessary.

10. Irrational belief: I should never feel anxious, sad, or angry.

    Rational belief: Emotions are natural and serve a purpose. It's okay to feel them without shame.

11. Irrational belief: I can't stand being rejected.

    Rational belief: Rejection is unpleasant, but I can handle it and grow from the experience.

12. Irrational belief: If I don't succeed at everything, I'm a loser.

    Rational belief: I can still be, and am, a worthwhile person even if I don't succeed at everything.

13. Irrational belief: I must avoid discomfort at all costs.

    Rational belief: Discomfort is part of life and growth. Avoiding it entirely limits my experiences.

14. Irrational belief: I can't be happy unless I have a partner, a great job, and recognition.

Rational belief: While these things enrich life, my happiness is not dependent on them. I can find joy in many areas, including from within.

15. **Irrational belief:** I can't cope with high stress; I'm overwhelmed and doomed.

    Rational belief: Stress is challenging, but I've coped before and can do it again.

16. **Irrational belief:** I must take responsibility for other people's problems.

    Rational belief: I can be supportive, but I'm not responsible for fixing everything for everybody.

17. **Irrational belief:** If something bad might happen, I shouldn't take the risk.

    Rational belief: Taking calculated risks is a part of life. I can prepare for setbacks and still move forward.

18. **Irrational belief:** If I feel it, it must be true.

    Rational belief: While my emotions are important, they don't always reflect the full truth. I can challenge my feelings with evidence.

The upshot is that when I find myself out of the zone—off-center—I try to pay attention to what I've been telling myself that made me upset, and I reframe it in a more constructive, rational way. I find this extremely effective. The process is similar to, but not the same as, techniques I later learned by studying cognitive behavioral therapy.

Cognitive Behavioral Therapy (CBT)

Aaron Beck is the father of CBT, which is widely considered to be a gold standard for helping people free themselves of problematic thought patterns, learned behaviors, and core beliefs.

> I'm always ready to change my beliefs based on new information.

What I learned from CBT is that we're all born with schemas—cognitive frameworks that shape how we interpret the world. Core beliefs are part of schemas; so are behaviors and emotions, which are often developed during childhood. These schemas act as prisms through which a person interacts with life. Anything that fits neatly into a schema's structure passes through it and is accepted. Anything that contradicts the schema tends to get filtered out. Over time, this can lead to cognitive distortions in how a person thinks, especially when the schemas are rigid and overfiltering or negative to begin with.

Beck was trained as a Freudian psychoanalyst, so when he noticed something that Freud hadn't mentioned, he was intrigued. His patients appeared to be disturbed not by unconscious processes but by automatic thoughts—those rapid, knee-jerk responses that trigger emotional reactions. From this, he deduced that automatic thoughts usually reflect a person's core schemas. Most people aren't aware of their automatic thoughts because they happen spontaneously; the brain treats them as facts. However, Beck realized that it's possible for a person to identify the automatic thoughts and reframe them in a more accurate or helpful way.[2]

> **Great mentors rewire how you see the world.**

So how do I use Beck's breakthrough to recenter? When I'm out of the zone, it's usually because I'm upset—anxious, very sad, or angry about something. There are a couple of ways I can approach this. I might use Albert Ellis's method and ask, *What am I telling myself right now? What is my irrational belief that I need to reframe?*

Or I might use Beck's method and ask, *What automatic thoughts are going through my mind? Was my reaction unwarranted because it was warped by my schema?* You can see what I meant earlier when I said that the frameworks of Ellis and Beck are similar but different. They share an objective that's very important to the concept of centering: Irrational and distorted thoughts must be reframed in a constructive way to engage with life more validly and happily. In short, to use a core tenet of CBT popularized by Beck and others, "The way you think affects the way you feel."[3]

CBT taught me how my interpretation of a situation—through automatic thoughts—can skew my emotions and behaviors. It also gave me an incentive to consciously question my negative thoughts. Here are 10 examples of distorted thinking that may be taking you out of the zone, followed by ways to reframe them to help get you back in:

1. **Distorted thought:** I didn't do this perfectly; therefore, I'm a total failure.

   Reframed thought: I didn't do this perfectly, but I did it well enough. I'll keep getting better.

2. **Distorted thought:** I messed this up. I always screw things up.

   Reframed thought: This one didn't go as planned, but I've done well before, and I can learn from this.

3. **Distorted thought:** My boss didn't compliment me. She must be disappointed or angry with me.

   Reframed thought: Maybe she was distracted. Instead of guessing, I'll ask her.

4. **Distorted thought:** They said I did a great job, but they were just being nice.

   Reframed thought: They didn't have to say anything at all. Maybe I really did do a good job.

5. **Distorted thought:** Sure, I contributed to our team's success, but it wasn't a big deal.

   Reframed thought: What I did mattered—it made a difference, even if it felt small.

6. **Distorted thought:** My gut tells me this is going to go badly.

   Reframed thought: I'm not a fortune teller. All I can do is prepare and give it my best.

7. **Distorted thought:** I got a bad performance review; my future is ruined.

   Reframed thought: It's just one review; it's disappointing but not the end of the world. I can recover.

8. **Distorted thought:** I feel like a failure, so I must be one.

   Reframed thought: Feelings aren't facts. Just because I feel this way doesn't mean it's true.

9. **Distorted thought:** I forgot to complete a task. I'm such an idiot.

   Reframed thought: I made a mistake; it doesn't define who I am.

10. **Distorted thought:** One person was on their cell phone during my presentation, so I could tell everyone was bored with me.

    Reframed thought: Sure, one person was on their phone, but others were engaged. I can't let one person outweigh the rest.

Dialectical Behavior Therapy (DBT)

Marsha Linehan created DBT, a trailblazing psychotherapy that draws from both CBT and mindfulness. Linehan nailed it with the idea of radical acceptance. Despite how it sounds, radical acceptance doesn't necessarily mean resigning yourself to what's happening or giving up entirely. It's about acknowledging the reality of the moment without arguing against it, to put yourself in a constructive mindset. I went to a number of Linehan's DBT training events years ago and studied how those therapists communicated with each other and their patients. It was amazing how present they were—no judgment, no rushing to fix or control anything. They were just intensely there, listening. That kind of presence changes everything, and it can be learned.

> **A dialectical approach means viewing something from multiple perspectives and interpreting it in different ways that are all valid.**

Linehan offered a blueprint for staying centered in the middle of the chaos. She categorized human psychology in three ways: the impulsive and reactive *emotion mind*, where thoughts and behavior are controlled by emotions; the detached and analytical *reasonable mind*, where thoughts and behavior are controlled by logic; and the *wise mind*, which is the balanced integration of the emotion mind and the reasonable mind: calm, intuitive, and centered.[4]

Linehan called her therapy "dialectical," meaning examining something from multiple perspectives. She found this to be the key to thinking in a more balanced way. She took a two-pronged approach to reframing an irrational or distorted thought: first, validate the belief as much as possible; then challenge it from different perspectives and find a middle path. The middle path harmonizes whatever truths can be found in both the belief and an alternative explanation. This approach tends to act as a stabilizer—no attempt to remove stress from the equation, at least at first. Just observation, never judgment, to better understand it.[5]

There was a time when someone close to me was struggling with suicidal thoughts. I couldn't understand it because I've always been the kind of person who wants to live forever. I just couldn't wrap my head around wanting to end it, so I started reading. I came across Linehan, and it was like a flashlight in a dark cave. Her insights helped me understand what hopelessness really feels like and how to be present with someone who's in that place. That didn't just help me support someone else; it helped me grow as a person, a leader, and a listener.

Linehan's core DBT principles of mindfulness, emotional regulation, distress tolerance, and interpersonal effectiveness gave me powerful tools to manage my emotional intensity. They've proven to be particularly helpful in high-stakes business scenarios, like complex negotiations or crisis situations. It's also a useful way to stay centered, and if I slip out of the zone, I can find my way back. Linehan wasn't about getting people to bliss out on a mountaintop. Her work turned mindfulness into a set of practical skills: observe, describe, participate.

Positive Psychology

The fourth technique in my recentering toolbox is positive psychology. It was founded in the late 1990s by Martin Seligman and colleagues. Unlike REBT, CBT, and DBT, which often focus on reframing unhelpful ways of thinking, positive psychology emphasizes human strengths, resilience, well-being, and optimal functioning. Instead of just asking, "What's wrong?" it asks, "What's right, and how can we build on it?"

> Don't merely tolerate adversity. Embrace it, and capitalize on every circumstance, especially setbacks.

Here are 10 positive psychology questions that my executives have found work well when encouraging team members to communicate:

1. What are my top strengths, and how can I use them more intentionally this week?

2. What is a goal I care about, and what obstacles could I face in achieving it? How can I navigate them?

3. When has our team been at its best, and what made that possible?

4. What is a moment at work when I felt fully alive or proud, and why?

5. If a teammate were in my shoes, how would I talk to them with compassion? How can I give myself permission to "be human"?

6. What gives me the most meaning in my role, and how can I do more of it?

7. What are three good things that happened today, and why did they happen?

8. What small act of kindness can I do for someone on my team today?

9. Who on the team am I grateful to be associated with?

10. What sincere praise can I offer one of my colleagues?

Mindfulness

Mindfulness is a powerful and uplifting approach to life. It involves radically accepting yourself, others, and the world—nonjudgmentally and unconditionally—without trying to change a thing. And it requires intentionally paying attention to what's happening in the moment. When I do that, I feel more peaceful and grounded, even in the middle of pandemonium.

In addition to Linehan's DBT, I learned the mindfulness techniques of Thích Nhất Hạnh, a Buddhist monk also known as Thay, and of Jon Kabat-Zinn, a molecular biologist and educator.

Thay taught mindfulness as the practice of easily noticing what's going on, using simple phrases like "Breathing in, I calm my body. Breathing out, I smile."[6] Thay's approach brings a beautiful clarity to the idea of mindfulness. Instead of treating it like an esoteric practice, his teachings show how mindfulness can be woven into the most ordinary parts of life—walking across a room, eating a tangerine—everyday actions that become meaningful when you're fully present for them.

Thay's mindfulness techniques aren't about achieving some perfect state; they're about creating habits that bring you back to yourself. This really resonates with me, especially in my career. When your mind is in a good place, you're a better leader, you think more clearly, you make better decisions, and you communicate more effectively. Mindfulness, the way Thích Nhất Hạnh taught it, is deeply human and calming. It helps me return to my center.

In the 1980s, Jon Kabat-Zinn translated mindfulness from the Buddhist monasteries to a secular form that dovetailed with Western medicine. He developed simple, practical exercises to help people manage stress and stay mentally clear, creating what he called mindfulness-based stress reduction, or MBSR.[7] His method was elegantly straightforward: Pay attention to the present moment without judgment and without trying to change it. That's all. By systematically directing the mind to each part of the body and practicing mindful breathing, as well as slow, intentional movement, MBSR trains the mind to anchor itself in the here and now for mental clarity. Kabat-Zinn didn't invent mindfulness, but he made it accessible to the modern world.

Mindfulness is also a tool for emotional regulation. When something is going haywire in an M&A transaction or I'm dealing with any of the myriad challenges that inevitably land on a CEO's desk, I practice mindfulness to get back into the zone. In a way, it's the easiest recentering tool in the toolbox because it requires no real effort at all. In fact, it's a process of *not* resisting, *not* expending energy, but simply experiencing something fully. At the same time, it's not static. It's deeply present and aware, paired with a heartfelt appreciation for the moment. I believe that's the secret to radiating personal charisma: the simple but rare combination of focus and gratitude.

One of the most powerful things I can do as a business leader is be fully mindful of the person I'm with in that moment. It could be a customer, shareholder, teammate, vendor—anyone. When I give a person my complete attention, I'm treating that encounter as something meaningful and that person as someone important. Both of those things are true. Sometimes I think to myself how fortunate I am to be right here, right now, with this person or group. This exact constellation of people will never come together in quite the same way again.

While I don't profess to know the scientific basis of it, my subjective experience is that mindfulness has a therapeutic, balancing effect. It helps me find equilibrium. The act of experiencing something fully with my mind, without trying to change it, is calming and liberating. It also helps me find stasis, or balance.

So those are the five frameworks in my recentering tool-box. If I get thrown off-center, I reach for one or more of them: REBT, CBT, DBT, positive psychology, or mindfulness. The techniques overlap, and sometimes I mix and match them. But the goal is always the same: to get back to center. It's not about eliminating problems, since they're part of the gig, but about responding to them intentionally from a grounded place.

I don't pretend to have it all figured out. I slip up sometimes, like when I catastrophize or catch myself demanding perfection from myself or others. But I pick up on it faster now, and I reframe it faster. I return to the zone more smoothly. No one stays perfectly centered all the time, but knowing how to get back to center will help you to navigate the ups and downs of life and business.

CHAPTER 3

Choosing the Right Industry to Consolidate

WHEN PEOPLE ASK ME how I ended up choosing the building products distribution industry for QXO, they assume I have some special affinity for lumber or roofing. The truth is it's not about the lumber; it's about my checklist of must-have industry traits.

After I stepped down as CEO of XPO in 2022, I spent more than a year examining nearly 600 companies across 55 industries. I was searching for the one that met all five of my requirements: immense scale, inherent long-term growth, a fragmented landscape ripe for M&A at favorable multiple arbitrage, economies of scale, and tech backwardness. "Tech backwardness" may sound negative, but it's actually positive because I can create a tech-forward industry leader that outpaces tech-lagging competitors.

> Formulate a bold yet attainable strategy that meaningfully benefits from long-term trends.

Every industry I've entered over the last four decades has nailed my trait checklist. If they had been missing even one of these characteristics, it would have been much harder for me to create dramatic shareholder value. You can use this same framework to pick your own industry, adjusting for your targeted scale, and the concepts will be relevant to your strategy. Here's a closer look at how I analyze my must-haves.

To Build a Big Company, Find a Big Industry

Before I look at growth trends, fragmentation, economies of scale, or technology, I first look at an industry's size. Without a large enough total addressable market (TAM), it's nearly impossible to create the revenue growth and operational scale needed to deliver on a big vision. With QXO, our sights are set on building a $50 billion business, so that eliminated industries with TAMs of $25 billion or even $100 billion. We focused on analyzing big trends in industries that have at least hundreds of billions of dollars of total market size—ideally closer to a trillion. Building products distribution is right in our sweet spot at about $800 billion.

> Scalability is one of the first things
> I study in a business plan.

Why is scale so important? Because you can't capture the entire market. A $50 billion company in an $800 billion industry holds about 6% market share. That's a significant percentage in any industry but still achievable. If the TAM is too small, a growth-oriented company is going to run into diminishing returns pretty quickly. This devolves into battling fiercely for every percentage point of market share while increasing the risk of antitrust regulation. Competition intensifies, and the major players in the industry start chasing diminishing returns. I'd rather choose an industry that's big enough to build a huge highly profitable business and still have room to grow.

I think of TAM as the playing field, and our team has the ball. We need enough room to maneuver without running out of space and the leeway to make occasional missteps without losing market share. In a smaller industry, even minor errors can feel catastrophic. But a sprawling industry lets us flex our M&A muscle, execute a tech-forward playbook, and still have plenty of blue sky above us.

There's one other thing related to scale that's always on my radar when I research industries: making sure the industry fundamentals reward scale, meaning structurally, bigger must truly be better. In every industry I've chosen—energy, waste management, equipment rental, transportation and logistics, building products distribution—size has delivered tangible competitive advantages.

For one thing, we can use size to drive significant economies of scale, including lower procurement costs, better pricing, and streamlined logistics. This, in turn, improves productivity, accuracy, and operational efficiency. For example, a denser distribution network equates to faster deliveries and lower transportation expenses, as well as better customer service. If we can become the industry's lowest-cost provider *and* its customer service leader, that's a double win.

Scale also delivers higher cash generation, which we can invest in technology that's too costly for smaller players. Cutting-edge enterprise systems, automation, and AI-based tools become exponentially more valuable when deployed across many thousands of transactions. In my experience, transformative technology is the single most important lever for revenue and margin growth, which is why it's central to our integration playbook. I give real-life examples of this in Chapter 7.

Identifying Growth Potential

Next, I analyze the TAM's inherent long-term potential for organic growth. That's the second nonnegotiable trend on my checklist. What are the industry's sustainable tailwinds? If it's already a growing industry, I want to see a healthy expansion rate before I enter because one company on its own, except in rare cases, can't force faster growth. An environment of organic growth means I can show up Monday morning at seven o'clock and already have built-in momentum: more customers, higher demand, better pricing power. If an industry is stagnant or shrinking, no amount of clever M&A or operational wizardry is going to overcome the headwinds. Companies in that scenario are just fighting to stand still.

The beauty of organic growth is that it compounds naturally. If you choose an industry that's expanding steadily, you'll have the luxury of reinvesting cash flow into the business—not just for technology but also to opportunistically pursue more M&A and attract more talent. Also, if you're riding the right growth wave, you can mess things up occasionally and still move forward. Picking an industry with built-in tailwinds for organic growth increases your chances of success.

Identifying growth trends is one thing; verifying that they have staying power is something else entirely. When I'm assessing an industry for long-term, secular tailwinds, I don't rely on gut feelings or pitch decks—I go deep. That means gathering an enormous amount of data, analyzing it from every angle, and pressure-testing it with people who have spent decades in the industry in various roles. I want to know not just whether the TAM is growing but why it's growing, how sustainable that growth is, and what could derail it over the next 10 or 20 years. Is the demand discretionary or non-discretionary? How resilient is it to economic downturns? Those answers matter a lot.

Another thing to consider is whether the long-term growth trend is more positive in certain parts of North America, Europe, or other regions of the world. In recent years, I've downplayed my dealings outside of North America and

Europe for a couple of reasons. For one thing, those business environments are often opaque. I also don't have a good enough feel for the geopolitics and macroeconomics of individual countries within those broader regions. Even within North America or Europe, some countries clearly have stronger growth prospects than others.

I believe that the United States will likely be the fastest-growing economy over the long run. Our markets are mostly free, with an adequate level of regulation—less regulation than in many other developed nations. Taxes are reasonable, and while the federal government changes every four or eight years, overall, it's a pro-business environment with laws that prioritize growth. I've also liked growing businesses in Europe. It's a huge economy overall, with dense markets for goods and services and well-developed rules of law. But Europeans work fewer hours per year than Americans, and that impacts gross domestic product (GDP). In addition, the social costs of running a business are much greater in Europe than in North America, including steep payroll taxes and employer contributions to national healthcare systems.

If I had my eye on an acquisition in Europe these days, I would want a purchase-price valuation at a lower profit multiple because long term, the GDP growth rate in Europe is likely to be below that of the United States. It's possible that

Europe's aggregate GDP growth rate could be one-half to two-thirds the rate of GDP growth in the United States over the next decade or two. In any case, Russia is likely to remain an unstable factor with murky ambitions in Europe.

This is all a prelude to a simple but crucial question: Does the industry I'm contemplating have favorable socioeconomic and regulatory factors, and is its growth being driven by consistent demand? The last thing I want to do is catch the top of a fad. If the growth is real and I've validated it from every possible angle, only then do I start getting serious. The choice of an industry plants a flag in the ground for investors and other stakeholders, so I make sure I get it right.

Fragmentation Is Your Friend

The next thing I look for is fragmentation—an industry packed with smaller players where no single company dominates. This creates an environment rich with opportunities for M&A. Most of my career success has come from acquiring businesses, improving them, and growing them to realize the significant economies of scale I mentioned.

If an industry isn't ripe for consolidation, optimization, and organic growth—the trifecta of my M&A strategy—I look elsewhere. I also stay away from sectors where private company valuations sit too close to public company multiples. What I look for here is meaningful multiple arbitrage—acquiring businesses at valuations well below my own, which, in my view, is the most important driver of successful M&A.

> A fragmented industry is an open invitation to build substantial value through M&A.

The cardinal sin of M&A is overpaying, whether because management falls in love with the deal or feels pressured into it. My acquisition team always talks to numerous targets at once to ensure we have alternate deals in the pipeline. The value-creation model doesn't work unless each part of the puzzle is locked in: We're paying a reasonable price, we can expand margins through continuous operational improvement, and we can grow the top line organically at a rate that outpaces the market. The purchase price is the invested capital (IC) in return on invested capital (ROIC), with the return being a function of both operational excellence and long-term industry tailwinds.

> Overpaying for an acquisition is the
> biggest mistake an acquirer can make.
> It destroys shareholder value.

Tech Backward Is the Path Forward

The final must-have on my checklist, and one that's especially exciting to me, is finding an industry that's somewhat tech backward. This may sound counterintuitive—shouldn't I want to jump into an industry that's already benefiting from the latest technologies? Actually, it's the opposite. If the companies that will be my competitors are already tech savvy, where's my edge? I don't want to compete on someone else's playing field, where they already have the advantage. I want to walk into an industry where the cool, mission-critical technology has been overlooked and businesses are still using Excel spreadsheets and gut instinct to make critical decisions. These industries—and some of them are huge—are ripe for disruption. The implementation of cutting-edge technology can immediately catapult a new entrant ahead of its competition.

When I say "tech backward," I'm not just talking about outdated websites or clunky point-of-sale software. I look for industries where I can apply automation, analytics, and AI and give my team a multiyear head start. Some of the best returns we've generated came from acquisitions that weren't sophisticated at all when we bought them. We deployed tools for pricing, logistics, inventory management, demand forecasting, customer management, procurement, and workforce planning, and the economics dramatically improved.

> **Look for tech-backward sectors with sizable markets hungry for efficiencies.**

My experience in the industrial sector has taught me that warehouses are one of the most under-optimized parts of many old-school industries and one of the fastest ways to create value through technology. I've bought companies where inventory is tracked on paper, where workers spend much of their day trying to find the right products, and where space is wasted because slotting is random instead of strategic. Customer relationships are merely transactional as a matter of necessity. These kinds of inefficiencies represent raw potential for an operator who knows how to fix them.

Bring in a proper warehouse management system, automate the slotting and picking processes, and introduce robotics and sensors for real-time tracking, and suddenly you're not just saving time; you're improving accuracy, safety, and throughput. Tech turns a warehouse from a cost center into a margin booster through better inventory visibility, faster fulfillment, and fewer mistakes, all of which also improve the customer experience. Beyond warehousing, there are huge opportunities to innovate across the entire value chain: B2B e-commerce, dynamic pricing, automated inventory management, route optimization for delivery fleets, and customer-facing tech that integrates ordering and fulfillment, to start.

In a nutshell, becoming the most tech-forward player in a space makes you the disruptor, not the disrupted. Assuming the industry fundamentals are sound, the more tech backward the industry is, the more value you can create by modernizing it. I've seen the earnings power of this strategy firsthand—and there's a pride that permeates the organization when you're the tech leader.

The Runners-Up

When I was evaluating potential industries for QXO in 2022 and 2023, several caught my attention but ultimately fell short. Exchange-traded funds (ETFs) initially looked appealing. I thought I could roll up dozens of smaller ETFs—$500 million of assets under management here, a billion dollars there—and create an ETF juggernaut with $50 billion to $100 billion of assets. But when I got deeper into due diligence, it became clear that the economics weren't on my side. The acquisition multiples for the larger targets were too high, leaving little opportunity to realize meaningful spreads between the cost of capital and the use of capital for M&A. Overpaying is anathema to me, so the ETF industry didn't make the cut because it failed the requisite test of M&A pricing.

> **The surest way I know to create immense shareholder value is to buy businesses at valuations well below our own, and then drive revenue and margin growth in those operations.**

Another industry that intrigued me was long-only asset management firms, especially active managers with substantial scale. Initially, this appeared interesting because many targets were available at reasonable prices, some as low as 5x EBITDA. I could see it all—integrate several large firms and use cutting-edge tech to share insights across a global team—but the "melting ice cube" fundamentals were impossible to ignore. The active asset management model has ongoing headwinds, including fee compression and assets moving to passive funds. It failed the organic growth tailwinds test.

Oil and gas was another industry I gave serious consideration to, partly because I know it well from the decade I spent in the energy trading sector early in my career. Exploration and production targets were cheap when I did my analysis, sometimes trading at just 4x or 5x cash flow. The idea was tempting. I would buy active wells at low valuations, get all my money back in four or five years, and then effectively have a royalty stream for another 15 or 20 years. But when I spoke with potential investors—sovereign wealth funds and pension funds that had backed me before—they were adamant that ESG mandates and poor industry performance in recent years made oil and gas a nonstarter for them. This would severely limit my ability to raise external capital and consolidate at scale. So despite my expertise in the sector and promising returns, oil and gas got the boot because I couldn't see how I'd fund the M&A machine.

A fourth industry I looked at closely was convenience stores attached to gas stations. On the surface, it had some of the right ingredients: a large TAM and tons of mom-and-pop operators in a fragmented landscape. It seemed ready for consolidation, and I also liked the cash flow generation. But as I thought more about the long-term trends, one question kept resurfacing: What happens when people stop driving gas-powered cars? Or stop owning cars altogether? Convenience stores depend on foot traffic, and there's a potential scenario—not next year, but eventually—where autonomous, electric, and shared fleets dominate personal transportation. In that world, people won't be grabbing a coffee and snack when they stop at a gas station to fill up. The prospect made me uneasy enough to take the industry out of contention— not because they're a bad choice today but because I don't know whether they'll be a good business 10 years from now.

> Getting the trend right is more important than getting every little decision right.

Each of these runner-up industries was compelling in isolation, and I'm certain that lots of money will be made by someone. But they failed to satisfy one or more critical items on my checklist, and one thing I've repeated a zillion times is that you can do a hundred things right, but if you get the major trends wrong, it's tough to make money. By sticking faithfully to the checklist criteria, my teams and I have avoided costly mistakes and executed our playbook for billions of dollars of value creation across industries.

For QXO, only one industry checked every box and finding it took more than a year of painstaking research and analysis. My advice? If you want to succeed big, don't compromise on any element of the industry evaluation. Choosing the right playing field is the first mission-critical decision you'll make when building a business from scratch.

CHAPTER 4

Raising Tons of Money

I'M A BIG FAN of capital markets. My teams and I have utilized them to fuel our growth strategies for decades. We've raised about $50 billion in total capital to fund M&A and organic growth, drawing on the smartest of the "smart money" from around the world and working with every investor category: ultra-high-net-worth family offices, private equity funds, sovereign wealth funds, pension plans, university endowments, long-only mutual funds, retail investors, passive ETFs, and hedge funds, as well as my own friends and family. There are pros and cons to raising money from each of these investor types, and a lot depends on where you are in the maturity of your company. In this chapter, I'll lay out how I think about sourcing capital and how to stay aligned with your major investors once they're on board.

> Growing a business from zero revenue to tens of billions is extremely gratifying. Creating massive shareholder value along the way is even better.

Before going into detail, I want to acknowledge the group that commits most of the capital and underwrites most of the risk in public companies—the holders of common stock. Retail and institutional investors together own every public company. Corporate leadership teams are the stewards of that money—we're charged with utilizing cash in intelligent ways to substantially increase value over time. To do that, our decisions have to be made through the lens of ownership even though management and the board are not necessarily the majority owners themselves. It's important to keep this responsibility in mind as you set out to sell part of your company to raise capital.

> The moment someone wires money into
> your business, you become their fiduciary.
> Treat that responsibility as a sacred trust.

Why I Like Being Public

I like running publicly traded companies. Being public makes it easier to build something big and lasting, at least for me. It gives me deep access to capital markets on non-onerous terms. No coupons, no covenants, and usually no board seats. In a matter of days, or even hours, my team and I can raise hundreds of millions, or even billions, of dollars in equity. Three days after we close, the money is in our account. Large public market transactions are intensely satisfying, and by allocating that money wisely, our track record paves the way for future rounds.

There are more advantages to being a public company than just funding. For one thing, it keeps your management team sharp. Every 90 days, the quarterly earnings release is a public report card for all to see. We share our perspective on the quarter, and analysts model our decisions in real time, poking holes in the results. That's fair—results that repeatedly hit or exceed the mark can earn a higher valuation multiple, so investors naturally want to know what's driving those numbers. The market rewards high performers in the share price, which in turn generates more currency to grow.

> **Always remember that your company's mission is to give shareholders back a lot more money than they gave you.**

Being public is also a form of free marketing. Some companies spend millions on brand awareness campaigns, whereas a stock ticker symbol does a lot of that for you. The visibility helps align your stakeholder base of shareholders, customers, employees, and suppliers, along with job candidates and M&A prospects. I've had acquisitions come to the table because someone saw our earnings report or read a note from a sell-side analyst. While most of the investors in QXO are repeat investors from my previous companies, two of our current top 20 shareholders had never heard of me until I was profiled by David Senra on his *Founders* podcast. We only came to his attention because we're a public company.

The elevated profile that comes with being a public company is not all sunshine and roses, though. It also requires a thick skin. No matter how well a company performs against outlook, there will be loud doubters in the wings telling the world why they think the stock is overvalued. I'm comfortable with that trade-off.

Dilution Should Be Strategic

Trading equity for capital sounds like pure upside until you realize you're selling off chunks of your company. New share issues dilute the ownership percentage held by existing shareholders. You're essentially trading ownership for fuel, and if you don't think through the math carefully enough, you can end up giving away too much for too little.

Say your company has 300 million shares outstanding. If you raise $5 billion at $20 a share, you're issuing 250 million new shares. Now you're at 550 million shares outstanding. This has a direct impact on the calculation of earnings per share, which is how the market ultimately values your business. You've changed the denominator on EPS, the primary metric that drives your stock price.

But dilution isn't inherently bad. If the new capital is deployed strategically to buy something that drives higher

profits per share, it's dilutive in the sense of percentage ownership, but it's accretive for your shareholders. If not, you'll
be going backward. Put another way, if you give up pieces of
the pie, you need to make the pie bigger, so everybody's slice
is worth more. I've diluted my own stock holdings plenty of
times over the years. I've gone from owning 90% of a company to 10%, but that 10% ended up being worth a whole
lot more than the original 90%. The capital influxes fueled a
much larger gain than the temporary loss from dilution.

Sources of Equity

There are some significant differences between the various sources that comprise capital markets. The source you
choose matters almost as much as the amount you get. Here's
how I categorize the main investor types.

Friends and Family

I've raised capital from all types of investors, but prior to
the launch of a new company with an unproven vision, the
options can be limited. I start with the people who know
me well enough to back me before the business is a reality—
mainly friends and family. They're not focused on valuation,

structure, or downside protection; they're betting on me. If I mess up, I'm going to have to explain myself to someone who knows my kids. That pressure is a small price to pay for the support of people who believe in you.

There's another reason I encourage entrepreneurs to bulk up on friends-and-family investors for a new venture: You'll be highly motivated to make good for your mother, brother, or best friend who signed up for the friends-and-family round. When other types of investors come later, that intense motivation will be baked into you.

Family Offices

Over the last 20 years, a new class of investor has emerged: the offices that manage the money of the world's wealthiest families. Family offices are often the first outside capital source I'll approach. The good ones are thoughtful, patient, and entrepreneurial. And they're more flexible than a traditional money manager, who's focused on beating a peer index by one or two percentage points. The family office investor wants long-term value and an asymmetric upside, where the potential for profit outweighs the potential for loss. They may be willing to tolerate more risk or volatility for a chance at a potential annual rate of return of 50% to 60%.

Unlike other institutional investors, family offices are usually not burdened by rigid investment mandates when making decisions. If they believe in a venture, they can move fast. They'll dig deep, ask sharp questions, and then wire the funds without needing to overdocument everything. That agility can be a major asset when a business is growing rapidly or sprinting to capitalize on a narrow window of opportunity.

Another advantage of family offices is that they're sometimes run by former operators or investors with real-world know-how about building businesses. They understand the grind and the unpredictable nature of early-stage growth. If you connect with the right family office, they can be valuable thought partners for you, offering strategic guidance and access to their network. In some cases, that warm intro to a strategic customer or ideal executive candidate can be more valuable than the capital itself. I've listed some of my favorite family offices in Appendix 5.

Private Equity

Private equity funds typically require structured investments that include dividend-yielding preferred shares and some governance rights, like board seats or veto power over strategic transactions, so I generally avoid taking money from them. However, I've made four exceptions, and all four have turned out very well. In 1999, when I was chairman and CEO of United Rentals, Apollo Global Management and what was then Chase Capital Partners invested about $1 billion in the form of two private investments in public equity (PIPEs).

The people from Chase were very low maintenance, and I only saw them once or twice a year. But Apollo got two seats on the United board and were very present in the business. They introduced us to a lot of important people, especially top-of-the-house connections at banks and institutional investors. They gave us market intelligence and business advice and had an active voice in our strategic decisions. More recently, we've had great experiences with two private equity funds based in Miami—Affinity Partners and Alpha Wave, both major QXO shareholders. Their managers also made useful introductions for us and contribute to the development of our strategy.

In general, though, I would advise against using private equity funds if you have the luxury to do so. As a group, they're entrepreneurial but can be fair-weather friends, and their focus on self-interest can favor aggressive decision-making. That said, if you have an early-stage company and need to raise a lot of money, private equity firms can be ready check writers. Their business model is based on generating fees; they're in perpetual dealmaking mode, and there's a good chance they'll invest again after their initial round. They might even bring in their limited partners or other sponsors to coinvest. The negative is that they'll typically sell after five to eight years, and the market knows that.

Sovereign Wealth Funds

These funds are some of the best investors on the planet, but they're not easy to land. I've worked closely with sovereign wealth funds in Abu Dhabi, Singapore, and elsewhere. They're serious and professional investors, and they think in decades, not quarters. They also come with global networks and huge influence. They'll ask hard questions, but the dialogue is constructive. The downside is that they take a lot of time; you have to start cementing the relationship brick by brick long before you need the capital. Before they invest, they'll perform 360-degree due diligence—not just on your numbers but on how you think, how you lead, and whether you're the kind of person they want to partner with.

If you're building a company for long-term value creation and you pass the test, a sovereign wealth fund will stick with you. Their investment makes a statement that they're in it for the long haul. They become your power ally, and their backing can unlock opportunities you could never realize on your own. You'll find a list of my favorite sovereign wealth funds in Appendix 5.

Pension Plans

Pension plans are excellent sources of capital when you're looking for big checks and low drama. They're not after board seats or special terms—what they want are predictable returns over long horizons, which makes them a strong match for business models like mine that deliver value by compounding returns over time.

Pension plans are not speedy investors. Decisions typically have to be passed through consultants and layered approval chains of investment committees, board members, and trustees. It's a very methodical risk evaluation process, and the money doesn't move until every box is checked. But when they commit, their capital is sticky; they don't freak out during short-term market fluctuations. That kind of consistency is worth the slower ramp-up.

Pension plan fund managers are primarily concerned about two things: alignment between management and shareholders, and risk management. If you can clearly demonstrate a durable cash flow strategy and back it up with a credible track record, they'll take notice. My own experiences with several Canadian pension funds in particular have been excellent. These are serious professional investors who quietly anchor some of the world's most successful enterprises.

Endowments and Foundations

Endowments fall somewhere between pensions and family offices, and the top managers are very sharp. They think independently, and they understand long-duration investing. Their capital commitments aren't always enormous, but they're thoughtful. Some endowment processes move fairly quickly, and some are glacial. Plan to spend up to two years fostering a relationship while they study your business before deciding whether they'll invest.

Endowment managers also tend to be among the most intellectually curious investors you'll meet. They ask thoughtful questions, dig into the mechanics, and want to understand how the business works. They're not in the middle of the Wall Street deal flow, so their perspectives often come from fresh angles.

Long-Only Funds

When your publicly traded company reaches a certain scale—significant daily trading volumes, real revenue and earnings, and a substantial organization—you'll start to get attention from long-only institutional investors. Firms like Fidelity, Janus Henderson, Invesco, Federated, and Orbis manage billions or trillions of dollars, deploying that capital into companies they believe will grow and generate superior returns. They'll dig into your model, market positioning, margin profile, capital allocation history, and management credibility. If they like what they see, they can become foundational shareholders.

There are two catches: First, most long-only funds only invest in large, well-established companies, and second, their investment attention span has come to resemble that of a hedge fund. Thirty years ago, long-only funds would buy my company's stock and hold it for a decade. Today, some might hold it, but they're just as likely to sell it in a few months—that's a "long-maybe" in my estimation. Nevertheless, you're going to need good relationships with the major long-only players because they're probably going to be your second-largest source of capital eventually, after index funds. Appendix 5 has my list of notable long-only funds.

Retail

Retail investors are often overlooked, but they can be a powerful part of your shareholder base once your company is public. These individual investors come in through platforms like Fidelity, Schwab, E*TRADE, and Robinhood or through financial advisors at the big banks, like Morgan Stanley, Bank of America Merrill Lynch, Wells Fargo, Citigroup, and JPMorgan Chase. Together, financial advisors represent a vast pool of capital. If they believe in your business thesis, they may stick with you longer than the institutionals.

Retail investors have their own advantageous trait: They talk. They post on Reddit, share on X, and swap ideas in group chats and forums. If they're excited about a stock, they'll become online crusaders for your company. All that positive exposure can create value because it shapes perceptions about your company and reaches existing and prospective investors, customers, and talent.

Passive ETFs

I almost forgot to put exchange-traded funds (passive ETFs) on the list because they operate so far behind the scenes. But they could end up being your largest shareholders. I'm talking about BlackRock, Vanguard, State Street, and other index funds. There's no marketing to do with them; they'll quietly buy your stock and move your company from index to index as market cap grows. The key thing to understand about passive capital is that it's algorithmic. It flows in and out based on rules the ETF applies, including market cap, float, and inclusion criteria.

Don't expect to have a personal relationship with ETF managers; they're not into meetings, pitches, or dinners. They're not betting on your vision; they're buying exposure to an index. Whether you speak with them or not, their votes matter in proxy season, so at a minimum, it's worthwhile to have a dialogue with their proxy voting group.

Hedge Funds

This one I learned the hard way. Hedge funds will tell you they're long-term investors and go on about alignment and conviction. But in my experience, most of them flip the stock as soon as the share price goes up. My team and I put together some PIPEs to raise money for QXO—deals I thought were well structured. As soon as they were permitted to, the hedge funds we let in immediately sold out. In fact, one of them sold the stock the day *before* it was permitted!

Hedge funds aren't built for what my companies do. The

large, multi-strategy funds hire some of the brightest minds on Wall Street, but by and large, they're traders, not partners and not long-term holders. That's not a criticism; they have a business model, and it's not about loyalty or patience. They manage risk by the day, sometimes by the hour, and if they can lock in a quick gain, they will. They may nod along with your vision in a meeting, but when the stock pops, they will be sellers. This increases your stock's volatility and can hurt your valuation multiple.

Most hedge funds operate on a short-term horizon. They serve a purpose, though. If you want to move a large block of public stock quickly, hedge funds can step in and write the check. The value they bring to the table is in liquidity and sophistication—a capital source for tactical needs, not strategic alignment.

Debt

Issuing debt is a powerful tool for a public company. Unlike equity, it doesn't dilute existing shareholders because no new shares are created. The interest paid on debt is often tax deductible, making it a very efficient way to raise capital. Also, because debt must be repaid, it forces a company to be disciplined with its finances.

Like any other capital lever, structure is key. If your company is generating consistent cash flow and you have a firm handle on your numbers, you can get access to debt on attractive terms. Then, if you use that capital to fund profitable M&A or other high-return initiatives, it can multiply value well above your cost of debt. The trick is to not get overleveraged.

My companies usually target a debt leverage ratio of about 1x to 3x EBITDA. We might go higher temporarily for the right acquisition, but we like to bring it back down quickly. A conservative capital structure puts us in a position to be opportunistic, and we can finance the opportunity if we need to without stressing the balance sheet. I'd rather be slightly under-optimized on leverage and sleep at night than live quarter to quarter hoping nothing implodes.

There's also a timing element to it. When debt markets are buoyant and pricing is attractive, my finance team will refinance, extend maturities, and lock in low rates. When the markets are tight, we'll pause and let our business model generate cash organically.

> A management team's legacy is the wealth it creates for the company's shareholders.

Investor Relations

My approach to investor relations is straightforward: Do what you say you're going to do, and if that changes, be the first to say so. I haven't met an investor yet who has had a problem with that. On a more granular level, tell investors what's working, what isn't, and how you're going to fix the underperforming parts. Sophisticated investors can easily detect nonsense, and they don't reward it. What they do reward is clarity and results.

> The best investors don't just write checks.
> They open doors and sharpen your strategy.

We talk to investors regularly, but not a lot of them. Once a company gets to a certain size, there are usually only a few dozen existing and prospective investors who can move the needle on share price. We focus our outreach on long-term holders: the sovereign wealth funds, pension plans, top-tier family offices, and largest long-only funds. For the most part, these are the investors who best understand the value of our compounding model, and they have the discipline to let it play out. We've built deep, mutually beneficial relationships with long-term holders that stretch over years, in some cases decades. They rely on us to keep them informed and close to the business.

While we never disclose nonpublic material information, we want our key investors to understand where we are in our plan, where we think we are in the cycle, and what kind of returns we realistically expect to deliver by executing well. These are smart people managing billions of dollars, and they make excellent sounding boards. We tell them about our wins and challenges and ask what they're seeing in the market. Sometimes they'll point out something we missed.

There are a lot of different steps to this dance between a public company and its capital sources. Ultimately, it's about creating a resilient base that can support the scale of what you're trying to achieve. Who you take money from, when you take it, how you structure it, and how you communicate about it are strategic choices that ripple through the entire life of the business.

> The most consequential decision you'll make in business and in life is who you surround yourself with.

Stay disciplined, and choose your sources carefully. Build relationships with partners who think in years, not months—long-term investors who believe you can succeed and give you the space to execute. The nature of the capital you accept will define how agile you can be, so align with people who share your time horizon and appetite for risk. Above all, remember that when someone wires money into your company account, they're trusting you to turn it into substantially more. You own that expectation.

CHAPTER 5

Mastering the Integration Playbook

MOST ACQUISITIONS DON'T CREATE shareholder value. The reasons vary, but they usually stem from the acquirer either overpaying or failing to deliver on synergies for revenue growth and margin expansion. That doesn't necessarily mean the underlying assumptions were flawed. More often, results fall short of projections due to poor integration and optimization—two surefire ways to unravel potential.

There are probably only a few dozen CEOs who are truly knowledgeable about all the ingredients that make an acquisition successful. Names that stand out to me include

Ed Breen (DuPont), Larry Culp (GE), Dave Cote (formerly Honeywell), Marillyn Hewson (Lockheed Martin), Steven Rales (Danaher), and Nick Howley (TransDigm). These CEOs know how to turn an acquired business into a much more profitable operation by harmonizing strategy across the combined company, redesigning the organizational chart, assessing talent, aligning compensation, strengthening culture, and making sure that the right metrics guide decisions on pricing, procurement, tech, sales, and operations.

> If you're not substantially improving the companies you buy, you're just moving capital around.

As an industry consolidator, I stake my reputation on my ability to transform separate entities into a cohesive profit machine through integration. If I focused solely on buying businesses and neglected to integrate them well, my companies would be a shambles of local branches with old branding, tech silos, and teams that don't talk to each other. Operations that are left to linger for months or years under legacy structures limit their profit opportunities, yet it happens all the time. That's not true integration; it's merely financial engineering.

> In every acquisition, we ask: *What's working well? What could work better?*

When we complete an acquisition, we institute financial, operational, and cultural unity as soon as possible. The first step is simple but crucial: Ask questions, and listen closely. The answers often come from the front lines, where employees who have never been asked for their input reveal precisely what's working and what's broken. That's where we start— with respect for the wisdom already within the organization.

Day One

For most acquirers, integration begins the day a deal officially closes, but for my companies, that's too late. The gap between signing and closing is filled with uncertainty for the stakeholders of the business being bought. Employees wonder about their jobs, competitors look to poach talent and customers, and the customers themselves become restless. If this uncertainty is left to fester, it risks damaging the value of the asset.

I do something unusual: I negotiate explicitly for unrestricted access to the company from the moment we sign an agreement. Sometimes we're limited in how much preclosing contact we can have with customers or vendors for antitrust reasons, but immediate access to employees is an essential condition for us. This isn't commonplace in M&A. Lawyers and boards often push back, preferring a neat boundary between signing and closing. But once we agree on price, the immeasurable value of securing early entry makes it one of the few must-haves in our negotiations.

> We don't shoot from the hip with big changes when we integrate an acquisition. We listen first and then act decisively.

Early access lets us have substantive conversations with employees—and with customers and vendors if permitted. We hold town halls and team meetings and visit field operations. I conduct face-to-face interviews with the top executives of the entity we're acquiring. My team and I have our antennas up for talent so we can start to understand who to elevate in the organization (more on this in Chapter 6). It sets the tone for the entire integration process and smooths the transition by easing anxiety. The scary "blind date syndrome" is alleviated as employees, customers, and vendors see that we're serious about making this work. It turns a period of vulnerability into one of excitement about the future we're building together.

Regarding the timing of the process, I generally take the Band-Aid® approach and rip it off because I've found that the pros vastly outweigh the cons. Sure, there could be some kerfuffles when we do an integration quickly, but the sooner we get the operations running on our systems for enterprise planning, human resources, sales, and customer relationship management, the better. The same goes for business intelligence tools like digital dashboards and key performance indicators (KPIs). Our dashboards display performance data in a graphical way to erase the barriers between levels of financial and operational sophistication. Everyone gets the same point, without big swings in interpretation.

Town Halls

For many employees of an acquired business, a town hall can be as daunting as meeting a blind date for dinner. Will we turn out to be their soulmate or a dud? The town hall is where we introduce ourselves and our company to our new colleagues and let them do the same. We're very mindful of their mixed emotions: The company they've looked to for stability for years is suddenly being bought by an industry entrant they don't know. That's a lot to take in.

> An acquisition comes with talented employees full of untapped ideas. Ask them what they'd do to make the business better.

When QXO closed on the Beacon Building Products deal, we sent out a Zoom town hall invite to everyone with a Beacon email address within minutes of the press release going live. I was happy that 3,600 people—the overwhelming majority of those invited—showed up on three hours' notice. Instead of lecturing about ourselves from on high, I gave a brief introduction and moved right to Q&A. It's essential to give new employees an open mic to share what's on their minds, and we respond just as openly. This starts to create an environment of trust.

The town halls we run are far from polished presentations; in fact, being too slick can be a mistake. I make a point of being accessible, answering questions candidly without prescreening, and encouraging feedback. We garner a wealth of insights into issues that need our attention—often things that long-tenured managers have overlooked out of sheer familiarity. It's inspiring to see people who have never been asked for their opinion by an employer suddenly step forward and find their voice. The wheels start turning, and it changes the whole dynamic: *Our new boss is not just asking questions. He's really listening to the answers.* If you want to experience the value of being present in the moment, as I discuss in Chapter 2, hold a Zoom Q&A with the employees of an acquired company.

Our town halls don't stop after that first big get-together. In the months immediately following an acquisition, my management team and I will do dozens of smaller, more intimate town halls and on-site team meetings. These events are a strategic lever in the integration process. We break the ice with questions like these:

- What are we doing that should be stopped immediately?

- Where are we overinvesting or underinvesting in the business?

- What are we doing that annoys or delights our customers?

- What are our competitors doing better than we are? What are we doing better than them?

- Are we prioritizing the products and services our customers value most?

- Are we pricing fairly for the value we deliver?

- What are the biggest causes of waste or inefficiency in operations?

- Where are we understaffed or overstaffed?

- Are we a magnet for the best talent in the industry? If not, how can we change that?

- Are we giving people the tools, training, and support they need to succeed?

- Are we tracking the right metrics?

- Does your compensation structure incentivize you to keep doing better?

- How well are we executing against our strategy?

- Are we allocating enough resources to safety?

- Which functional teams have the highest and lowest engagement and why?

- What new technology capabilities do we need, and why?

- What are the biggest risks to achieving our goals, and how do we mitigate them?

- Are we making decisions fast enough, or have we become too bureaucratic?

This is when inherited issues usually come to light. We come away with a list of targeted actions that matter to our employees; these get turned into workstreams with named owners who are accountable for the deliverables. One of the things we listen for specifically is WOT-WOMs—an acronym for waste of time, waste of money. Employee time and company capital are finite resources, so we pay very careful attention to how we spend them. If a workstream doesn't contribute to above-market revenue or margin growth, either directly or indirectly, it's a WOT-WOM and an opportunity for us to flip it positive.

On a personal level, I make it a priority to connect directly with as many people as possible across the company, especially the frontline employees. For example, I'm eager to meet anyone who interacts with a customer, either in sales or support. I ask questions, scribble down notes, and always end by extending an invitation to email me directly. For many, it's the first time they've spoken to the CEO, and the enthusiasm it creates is palpable. It's gratifying to have a hand in beginning to shift the culture, and it's well worth my time.

> **When I acquire a company, I soak up every piece of information I can find. The more perspectives, the better.**

Employee Surveys

In my first book, I talk about why quarterly all-employee surveys are one of my absolute favorite tools for running a business. My integration team deploys a slightly tweaked version of this survey immediately after we buy a business. It sets a respectful tone and communicates an important message—that we want to hear the truth so we can act on it.

We're rewarded with a gold mine of actionable insights for improving everything from truck driver safety and pricing discipline to break room seating. The survey mechanism itself is conducive to thoughtful responses, as it gives employees time to reflect before answering, which isn't always possible during live Q&A sessions. We keep it simple with three key questions derived from the longer list: What's working really well? What needs fixing? What's your single best idea to improve the company? This lets us track trends over successive surveys. Employees at every level receive the survey if they have a company email address.

There are only two things a manager manages—return on time and return on capital—and getting employee feedback in both areas pays dividends. Our first survey of Beacon employees was sent out just days after we signed the purchase agreement, and it generated thousands of candid responses. My senior team and I read every one. Recurring themes emerged, both good and bad. We used AI models, word clouds, and sentiment analysis to analyze them in dozens of different ways. Then we factored their feedback into our plan, which ultimately zeroed in on the biggest profit opportunities.

From an efficiency standpoint, crisp surveys yield the best return on time of any mass employee feedback loop. The distribution and response processes are fully automated, and the response rate is usually high if you have an engaged organization. Realistically, in a large company, this quantity and quality of insights can't be harvested any other way. While we administer surveys throughout the year, a simple all-employee survey is a fantastic way to kick off an integration.

Early Integration

I believe in integrating a business methodically from the start. Once we've identified the hot issues through town halls and surveys, the next step is to determine the best way forward. The numbers will flag what to tackle first. Our initial analysis is geared toward clarifying three things: What's the fix, what's it going to cost, and what return will we get by fixing it? Integration is fundamentally about capital allocation—putting finite resources behind the initiatives that yield the highest return on invested capital. Everyone has their own pet projects, but not all projects are ROIC rockstars, and this is where discipline comes in.

We've all come across a business problem that appears urgent at first glance, but when the numbers are run, the solution isn't worth the cost. Then there are the sleepers, with hidden upsides that will be overlooked without proper scrutiny. Some items require deeper-than-usual analysis to project the ROIC; for example, precise returns on capital allocated to customer satisfaction and employee engagement are hard to pin down, but these investments can certainly facilitate revenue growth and margin expansion. By using data-driven analysis, we end up with a set of clearly defined prioritizations, milestone targets, and end goals. It keeps everyone focused on the things that move the needle.

> I never assume success is guaranteed.
> A healthy fear of failure sharpens execution.

From there, it's about consistent execution—and speed. In our playbook, speed is the key differentiator. Every project, decision, and workstream needs to move at maximum, controlled speed. We constantly ask, "How can we do this faster without screwing it up?" We drive until the hubcaps are rattling but not so fast that they're falling off. I'll share something you may find surprising: Micromanaging is usually not helpful in business, but when you're integrating an acquisition in an accelerated time frame, it's critical to maintain control.

To make sure we never lose sight of what matters most, we use a tracker. It's a detailed master spreadsheet that lists every integration and improvement initiative we're pursuing. A single integration can have thousands of specific line items, with each assigned a single "throat to choke"—an owner who's personally accountable for the outcome on a firm completion date. Every line is color-coded with a traffic light system: Green means on pace, yellow warns there's a risk of missing the deadline, and red means danger. When a tracker item flashes red, it jumps to the top of the list so the team can get it back on track.

Using a tracker may sound mechanical, but process is exactly the point at this stage, with the data collected, the analysis done, and the decisions made. Our management team meets to go over the tracker daily in the early weeks of an integration and at least once weekly in the months that follow. These meetings are partly to draw on the wisdom of the crowd and partly to keep everyone in the loop.

> **We build an organization where decisions flow cleanly, responsibilities are unmistakable, and results matter.**

Scientists don't fully understand the evolution of traits that support motivation, but our brains are reacting in part to signals in the environment. Group meetings, where the full tracker is up for discussion, give everyone a sense of what the landscape of the integration looks like, not just their line items. This is valuable context for decision-making, as well as mindset. Our managers take pride in turning reds and yellows into greens. Shifting problems to progress is part of the rhythm of our culture.

> **Big returns come from taking calculated, high-conviction bets.**

Methodical Transformation

Once the foundational pieces of the integration are secure, the real transformation can begin. This involves moving methodically through organizational redesign and operational integration through technology—two areas that can undermine ongoing value creation if you get them wrong. The next two chapters cover the key approaches my team and I use to fulfill the promise of an acquired business, step by disciplined step.

CHAPTER 6

Organizational Integration

THE FIRST QUESTION TO answer in organizational design is: *How is the business we're acquiring going to create value?* It isn't the real estate or inventory or customer list you're buying; those are just tools. The blueprint for money generation is ROIC, and that will largely be determined by your culture, organizational structure, and employee engagement. These three "people factors" have been the main drivers of my companies' ability to more than double the profit of acquired operations.

I'll start with the organizational chart: the hierarchical blueprint of well-run companies. Over the years, I've reviewed thousands of org charts, some elegant and efficient, others chaotic. I've found that the org chart is often a good indicator of a company's focus, including its cultural priorities and workplace environment. Get the people part right, and it can become your greatest competitive advantage. Get it wrong, and you'll spend years untangling dysfunction and losing money.

> To create billions of dollars of value, you need people who are brilliant, driven, honest, and have a good heart.

Designing the Optimal Org Chart

Somewhat counterintuitively, a great org chart isn't about the people per se. The business must run efficiently regardless of who is in the seats. Said another way, if the structure doesn't hold up without a particular individual, then the org chart doesn't work. When it's done properly, someone from outside the company can look at the chart and immediately understand how the company is structured without knowing any of the personalities involved.

I'm going to use an example of large-scale M&A here when talking about a full org chart redesign. Smaller acquisitions may only require modifications to your existing management structure, but even a modest change is an opportunity to examine your org chart for ways to improve it.

> **People commit when they understand the company's strategy, their role in it, and how they'll be rewarded for success.**

Here's how I approach it: I start by sitting down with a big printout of the acquisition's org chart as early as possible, preferably during due diligence. I really look forward to it. Some people do crossword puzzles; I do org charts. I've seen the full spectrum, from elegant, symmetrical designs to charts that remind me of a Jackson Pollock painting, with overlapping roles, dotted lines, and excessive layers. These are incoherent and bloated because no one's ever stopped to ask, *What is the optimal organizational architecture to accomplish our goals?*

Conceptually, the optimal structure is an organization where decisions flow cleanly, responsibilities are unmistakable, and results matter—and not in isolation. In any business, the organizational structure needs to work in concert with the operating model, so the decisions required to operate the model should inform the org chart design. At the heart of that design is this question: *Where should decision-making and P&L authority sit?* The answer always guides to a role, not a person.

I never feel constrained by an org chart's existing structure when making these decisions. The consequences of retaining past mistakes are huge. But I'm also mindful that any shift in the accountability model must be backed by solid change management. This includes providing clarity on new career paths when making deliberate leadership role adjustments. In addition, autonomy given to local leaders must be paired with strong governance, a new incentive structure tied to the right performance metrics, and guardrails to avoid unintended outcomes.

There's a lot to consider before getting into the process, and here's the caveat: *Always keep it simple.* If it looks like a bowl of spaghetti, it probably runs like one. A great org chart should fit on a single page—a clean, geometric structure with minimal dotted lines and no asterisks. Any one of your managers should be able to walk up to a whiteboard and draw it in two minutes.

Centralization Versus Decentralization

On a structural basis, decisions about P&L ownership typically reflect one of two organizational strategies: centralize or decentralize. Centralization consolidates control at the corporate or divisional headquarters. This makes it easier to realize advantages of scale and standardization, and it facilitates compliance with policies and procedures. But centralization can also slow decision-making and highlight disconnects between leadership and the field. By contrast, decentralization pushes authority out to the local leaders or to district or regional management. This is more typical of an entrepreneurial culture that places a high value on agility and accountability at the local profit-center level—but it can create cost inefficiencies and an inconsistent customer experience.

Corporate and shared services like human resources, finance, and technology are classic candidates for centralization. But with functional authorities, weighing whether to centralize or decentralize requires serious thought because the decisions come with trade-offs. Take procurement, for example: By pooling purchasing power, companies can negotiate better prices, leverage their scale, standardize quality, and strengthen strategic supplier relationships. The downsides are that a central team can be slow to respond to urgent local needs and, additionally, may overlook valuable suppliers who have cultivated local relationships. Replacing a long-standing supplier involves a significant risk to supply chain stability. To reap the benefits and mitigate the downsides, a balanced approach combining centralized and decentralized activities is crucial, with specific strategies addressing factors like product type and spend category.

The pricing function has significant ramifications. When pricing decisions are kept local, sales teams can respond quickly to changes in market dynamics. Typically, it's the local sales manager who has the best ear to the ground on supply and demand. The downsides of decentralized pricing are inconsistency and internal price wars that can erode margins.

A purely centralized pricing model enforces margin discipline and delivers a consistent customer experience. But central pricing teams can miss the subtleties of local demand unless they're armed with market insights from real-time data. To truly bridge this gap, it's critical to invest in a team of data scientists dedicated to analyzing market demand at the local level by product SKU, and at scale, across the entire operating geography.

Growth and Change

The whole point of org chart redesign is to structure the company as a bigger, better moneymaking engine than it was before. Instead of focusing on who holds what position in the legacy business, we'll begin by identifying where the value is created. As noted, this is key to org chart design. Some people may stay in their legacy role, and some may not. The right person in the right seat today could change with a future acquisition or expansion into new product markets. If it turns out there are two top-notch managers with expertise in the same area and only one slot, we'll let one of them go. A well-designed org chart accommodates changes like this without requiring a full redesign.

It takes commitment to let an org chart seat stay open until the ideal person is found. An empty slot is far less risky than filling it with the wrong person. My companies' org charts reflect what we want the organization to be, not what we've been handed to work with. We never compromise the structure to check a box, and we'll hire from outside the company if we need to. That may not sit well with some legacy managers, but it's the best thing for the organization. If I look at a business and see a Frankenstein org chart—an amalgamation of charts from prior M&A—it tells me that each leader has been allowed to keep their fiefdom intact to the detriment of the whole. That's integration in name only.

> A company that's creating outsized shareholder value will never struggle to attract top talent.

We use zero-based head count planning when redesigning org charts. Essentially, we take a fresh look at every position and categorize it as a must-have, a nice-to-have, or what-the-hell. And we're diligent about taking a broom to the third category. The nice-to-have category is a larger cost-reduction opportunity than either of the other two, so by keeping the most promising nice-to-haves and saying goodbye to the rest, we can optimize the head count. These choices can ignite some vigorous debate, but it's worth it. In my experience, addressing the nice-to-have category alone can improve profit by 10% to 40%.

A word of caution: Taking costs out of a business should be a meticulous process—thoughtful and analytical—not a free-for-all. It affects many people's lives. In addition, if you overdo it, it will hurt your customers and ultimately hit your P&L because most customers won't stick around to see if your service recovers.

> **Create a results-matter culture, and balance ambition with empathy.**

Spans and Layers

The central concept of org chart design is optimizing spans and layers. A manager's span of control is exactly that: their number of direct reports. I've seen companies where someone "manages" one person! That's not a span or even management—it's companionship—and it pains me to think shareholders are paying for it. On the flip side, I've seen spans where someone's had 30 direct reports. That's not management either—it's firefighting. When a leader is being pulled in different directions all day long, there's no time for coaching or strategy.

To some extent, the optimal number of direct reports depends on the business. In my companies, I've found the right number is somewhere between 7 and 14. That's enough people to justify the manager's salary but not too many to manage effectively, even in a fast-paced culture. It's entirely feasible to review deliverables with 7 to 14 people for 30 to 60 minutes each week. And with a team of this size, it's also feasible to hold productive group meetings.

> **Build a team that's passionately committed to achieving outstanding results.**

The same principles that apply to spans also apply to layers. Layers are the number of rungs between the person on the front line and the CEO. Every layer slows down communication and decision-making. The goal is to flatten the org structure—not to the point where no one knows who's in charge but flat enough so ideas move fast. I've seen org charts where there are nine layers between the customer and the CEO. That's bureaucracy. The shorter and more direct the line from problem to decision, the better.

It's immensely satisfying to adapt an org chart to a new acquisition, with the spans and layers streamlined like a high-performance machine. Everything improves—execution, culture, problem-solving—and the customer feels it.

Building the Right Team

I prioritize allocating substantial resources to talent evaluation. Within weeks of closing a deal, my team identifies the superstars—the A players, who are intelligent, driven, and aligned with our vision. They also pinpoint the B players, who are competent but may need coaching to excel or have been in roles that don't match their strengths. I've seen many B players turn into A players with the right training. These underutilized employees deserve the chance to prove themselves. However, in larger acquisitions, keeping all B players is rarely necessary, so we focus on retaining those with the greatest potential.

> Be decisive with people who aren't moving the company forward, and offer them a generous exit package.

The C players are the ones who don't buy into the vision or are dragging down the team. Experience has taught me to move swiftly with C players. Integrating an acquisition includes merging two cultures, and the last thing any company needs is subpar talent in the mix. We let the Cs go as soon as possible, but graciously, often with substantial exit packages. How you treat people when they exit sends a powerful message about the kind of company you're building. We can look the remaining employees in the eye and say with sincerity "We want you to stay and be part of our future." Nothing calms an organization down faster than this simple act of reassurance.

I had a wise chief operating officer, Wayland Hicks, when I was CEO of United Rentals. Wayland had previously been the COO of Xerox. He was fond of saying "A fish rots from the head," meaning if your leaders aren't top tier, their bad characteristics cascade downward, dragging performance with them. Typically, when we acquire a business, most of the people we exit don't come from the front lines; they're in the mid to upper echelons of the legacy operation. That's where we usually find most of the bloat.

Field organizations, especially at the branch level, are rarely overstaffed. They're closer to the customer and tend to be leaner, so there's less fat to cut. In fact, we often add head count in field sales or other customer-facing positions. But first, we make sure we get the leadership right because when the top of the house is dialed in, the rest of the organization will follow. Get it wrong, and, as Wayland would say, the fish will start to stink.

My teams have honed their processes for talent evaluation over hundreds of acquisitions. We use panel interviews, structured assessments, and rigorous benchmarking to ensure that our decisions aren't based on gut feelings or biases. The assessments are tied to the KPIs used in our business, and we stack-rank the talent accordingly. Each corporate leader—human resources, finance, sales, operations, technology—is responsible for identifying gaps and overlaps in their combined team. Who holds the critical relationships with customers and vendors? Which new employees have the strongest track records and performance appraisals? How did the legacy team perform relative to industry competitors? Where will the combined team need support? Using this framework, our corporate leaders begin to visualize restructuring their teams around the top performers.

During the evaluation period, I get briefings at least daily from my functional leaders, sometimes as a group on Zoom. Since most of them are in the field at this stage, it's valuable for everyone to hear firsthand what others are discovering. Group calls also help keep the energy high and encourage each leader to deliver results. Meanwhile, I'm keeping my ears tuned for people patterns that show up as the integration gets rolling—for example, a history of high turnover at a certain facility. Constant communication with HR leadership is key.

It's never a perfect process, but we remedy most of the gaps, overlaps, and glitches as part of our playbook. It's a great feeling to assemble a cocoon of very talented people who are all aligned, all trying to create tremendous shareholder value. As soon as we get everyone working coherently toward that goal, our odds of success increase significantly.

Demystifying Compensation

Once we've got our org chart nailed down and know who we want in each seat, we make sure the compensation plans incentivize execution on the profit improvement plan. Our compensation philosophy is that people should have an opportunity to make an extraordinary amount of money, but only if they deliver in a big way. I'm happy to "overpay" with a bonus if it means the person has made a major contribution to the success of our company. This feels like stating the obvious, but I've seen countless companies get it wrong. They tie compensation to metrics that don't drive customer satisfaction or shareholder value—or to metrics beyond the employee's control. Some companies overcomplicate incentive plans to the point where people don't know what they're earning or why. I recently acquired a business that had 76 different compensation plans for the same role!

Compensation should never be a mystery or a source of frustration. Each employee with an incentive plan should know precisely what they need to do to earn their bonus and be able to see how they're tracking throughout the year. For our most senior executives, the compensation plans have a big equity component tied to total shareholder return (TSR). At the end of every calendar year, we compare our stock's performance to the S&P 500 index. If we rank lower than the 55th percentile, the TSR-contingent compensation isn't earned, and it's permanently forfeited. We don't reward poor or even mediocre performance. If we can't outperform 55% of the S&P 500, then we really don't deserve that chunk of incentive compensation.

> **Invest generously in top talent, and tie their compensation to performance.**

It's motivating for employees at all levels to see their efforts rewarded. They work harder, smarter, and more collaboratively—and they're proud to be on a high-performing team. The impact compensation has on culture is the part so many companies miss: When a team hits its targets, it should trigger a wave of pride, as well as a financial reward.

Marrying Cultures

Countless books and articles have been written about the importance of company culture, stakeholders, and core values. I want to talk about how culture fits into successful M&A. An integration at any scale requires a sharp focus on culture, especially when it's part of a company's overarching plan to grow significantly. I'm currently in the process of consolidating the building products distribution industry with QXO, and we've set a $50 billion revenue target within 10 years. Everyone in the organization is signed on to that goal.

One of the fun things about doing lots of M&A is that it's like growing a family. Each new acquisition is like a new person in your life. When we buy a company, the goal isn't to replace its culture—we want to integrate the best aspects of both cultures to create a symbiotic organization. It would be indefensible to pay millions or billions of dollars for a business we didn't admire. We make sure we incorporate all those admirable parts into our combined culture.

Four things I consider to be imperative in a company's culture are honesty, a strong work ethic, accountability, and team collegiality. We use the cliché "teamwork makes the dream work" to reinforce a culture of us-us-us and not me-me-me. And there's a fifth imperative: respect. It's crucial to create a safe space where people can respectfully disagree and feel respected in return. Our culture encourages everyone to constructively challenge ideas, including my own. That's how we make great decisions. By contrast, a discombobulated culture that's toxic and disrespectful, with cliques at war, is like a cancer. I've bought a few companies like that because I needed other things they offered, and it took us a year or two to cure them.

In a large company, the culture vibe is driven by a few dozen people at the top of the organization. It's important to set the tone from the top down, always being careful not to force-feed the culture. When I founded QXO in 2024, the executives didn't pick the core values at headquarters and circulate a decree. Instead—you guessed it—we sent out a survey to every person in the company. We asked them what they thought our core values should be, and then we whittled that down to a handful of the most popular and sensible suggestions. This was followed by a second survey to see which values on the short list resonated with employees. Finally, we made sure the values QXO adopted aligned with the culture we wanted to build.

By the way, you'll know when you're sending out too many employee surveys because the response rate will dive below 50%. If you're asking relevant survey questions and sharing results, employees can see that you're taking their input seriously, and you should be getting a response rate of 70% or higher.

Brand Integration

Another impactful way to communicate culture is through branding. One thing that bugs me about a lot of consolidators is that they don't truly integrate the companies they buy. Most end up with a grab bag of brands. Why should legacy teams—and their customers and vendors—think of the parent company as a big, unified leader with a powerhouse value proposition when the optics say the opposite? Why should shareholders buy into it?

I've heard versions of this speech many times: "Brad, I know you typically change your acquisitions' names to your brand, but we're different. We've been in business for decades, and everybody knows our name. We don't want to lose loyal customers or employees." I respond, "I heard everything you said, and you have a lot to be proud of. But we're changing the name." We go to market under a single brand because the power of one brand is real. Everyone's marching to the same drum. Everyone knows where they fit in.

> A unified brand builds pride and unites
> the team around a singular vision.

We begin the rebranding process and handle all related logistics as soon as possible after an acquisition. I sometimes get asked whether it's really possible to weed out old brands in a very large company. The answer is yes—I had more than 150,000 employees at XPO before we spun off parts of the business, and a lot of those people came to us through the 18 acquisitions we integrated. But thanks to the hard work my team put in, XPO really does operate as one company, and each spin-off does the same. There's no line item for "unity" on a balance sheet, but there's enormous value in having a cohesive team.

Rebranding a large acquisition can be overwhelming, so we start with small things that are quick and inexpensive to produce. These include company-branded polo shirts and other swag, branded LinkedIn banners and screen savers. Within days of completing the acquisition, the legacy branches start to get window decals, floor mats, and signage to revamp their locations and vehicles. Salespeople get new business cards, and all employees switch to new email signatures and addresses, with forwarding from the old addresses. With preparation, the electronic rebranding can be set up to happen automatically, supported by the tech department.

High-speed rebranding can supercharge brand awareness because there's a wow factor: Markets sit up and take notice. It's also contagious. Branch managers take pride in refreshing their locations and share before-and-after photos of their store makeovers online. Employees post photos of their new swag on social media and share the news with customers, vendors, and peers: "I'm with a great company that's going to do big things in the industry."

As you execute your integration playbook, remember that the ultimate goal is to double the profit of the acquired business. You've created the most effective organizational chart and placed the right talent in the right seats. The team is part of a winning culture under a single brand, and they're committed to the vision. Now, the last big piece of the integration is the application of technology.

CHAPTER 7

Tech Integration

EVERY ACQUISITION COMES WITH operational systems, processes, controls, and assets. These components represent latent profitability that can be unlocked through operational integration—and the basis for world-class integration is technology.

Earlier, I noted that I like entering tech-backward industries if the other fundamentals are sound because my company can scoop the competitive advantage. There's good value in being the disruptor. But even if the business you acquire is tech savvy, you'll leave money on the table if you don't fully integrate the operations. That can only be done by applying advanced technology as the foundational basis for continuous improvement.

> The future of business relies on intelligent systems that streamline operations and enhance decision-making.

Technology is one of the largest investments I make for two reasons: Systems integration is the only way to fully unlock the potential of operational levers, and it provides an opportunity to build on that advantage. My companies have invested billions of dollars in technology to improve demand forecasting, procurement, inventory management, transportation and logistics, pricing, sales force effectiveness, e-commerce, and other critical applications. The emergence of AI is now making it possible for these areas to contribute even more strongly to financial and operational excellence.

Transitioning the Tech

The planning for systems integration starts once we've signed an acquisition agreement. These are some of the questions we ask the company's tech staff so we can begin conceptualizing the process:

- What enterprise resource planning (ERP) system are you using?

- What point-of-sale (POS) system is deployed in your branches?

- Do your field operators have real-time dashboards? What about the corporate leaders?

- How do you manage pricing?

- Do you have a centralized data lakehouse where you store and model data?

Nine times out of 10, the answers we get point to huge opportunities for optimization, starting with a single ERP system.

Any ERP transition comes with the risk of disruption, but it's vital to the integration. Once we move an acquisition to our ERP, we can see the numbers in real time and in the proper context. My teams have dealt with large acquisitions that were running as many as 35 different ERPs across their footprint—that's not a tech stack; it's a tech heap. No wonder some companies struggle to close the books at month-end and can't benchmark branches, forecast demand, or manage inventory with precision. I would argue that a mishmash of tech is as bad as no tech at all; at best, it's flying half-blind. This is why our integration playbook emphasizes one fully integrated tech stack across the combined company.

> **Integrate your tech stack so every part of the system talks to every other part.**

There will be pushback; people love their legacy ERP systems, even when they've been duct-taping them together for years. But there's no such thing as a high-performance business with five different general ledgers, 10 chart-of-account structures, and a scary tangle of half-integrated modules. This isn't the time to be sentimental. When we undertake a large transformative M&A integration, we're even open to changing our existing ERP if that's what's best for the new size and complexity of the business.

In parallel with the ERP transition, we'll overhaul the acquisition's POS system. This can be a big change for them, especially in industries like distribution, where the branch is the beating heart of the business. In many companies, the POS system is either outdated or isn't connected with the totality of the operations. We replace that with robust POS capabilities for dynamic pricing, controlled discounting, predictive inventory management, fulfillment, and transactional processing. Structured and unstructured data from all interactions flow into our data lakehouse, where they can be analyzed on demand using our business intelligence (BI) dashboards.

> The ability to pivot quickly is more valuable than perfect planning.

Cutting-edge dashboards are critical to realizing the promise of an integration—and by cutting-edge, I don't mean every bell and whistle. The presentation should be clean, focused, and actionable, not a jumble of 700 metrics that make your eyes bleed. Great BI design facilitates operational excellence, cost control, forecasting, asset management, and strategic line of sight, along with universal financial KPIs like revenue, margin, and free cash flow. The operational KPIs can vary quite a bit depending on the type of business you're in.

When I was in waste collection, the key operational metric was stops per hour. After a truck makes a certain number of pickups, the fixed costs are covered, and each additional stop has outstanding flow-through to the bottom line. In the construction equipment rental business, a national provider holds billions of dollars of rental fleet like a hot potato, so time- and dollar-utilization metrics are priority KPIs. In less-than-truckload (LTL) freight transportation, customers place a super-high value on low damage frequency and on-time delivery performance. They want to know what these numbers look like. In QXO's industry, building products distribution, customers measure the value of our service based in part on "on-time and in-full" (OTIF) performance. We use our dashboard to understand fluctuations in OTIF, looking at factors like product availability and distance to destination.

> Customer satisfaction is the natural result of a well-executed operational playbook.

Our curated dashboards are designed in-house and include 15 KPIs—that's it. Each KPI shows a black bar for a current goal adjacent to a colored bar showing actual performance in real time. Our managers can see at a glance where they're winning and where improvement is needed. We don't do meetings where people say "I think." We do meetings where people say "Here's what the numbers show" and talk about the dashboard data.

The source of all this intelligence is sitting behind the scenes: our systems architecture and centralized data lakehouse. This repository pulls structured and unstructured data from across the stack—sales, inventory, pricing, logistics, customers, procurement, e-commerce—everything lands in the lake. From there, we model, cleanse, and analyze the data.

> A modern operation doesn't guess at logistics;
> it models, tracks, and calibrates in real time.

Think about how powerful this is in terms of M&A integration, particularly when a massive amount of legacy transactional data is added to the lake. Want to know the year-over-year profitability of a single branch by SKU or seasonality? Or forecast demand based on historical weather data? Or identify the branches that are discounting too much? These are all examples of BI using structured data modeled with company- and industry-specific precision. We're now able to train AI agents to become deeply familiar with our business model and markets, generating actionable insights. We use this information in combination with our channel visibility to create campaigns that drive demand.

I believe the process of unifying an acquisition with our tech stack is the single most effective way to unlock not just efficiency but also new ways to differentiate our offering. And it can extend avenues for value creation far beyond traditional horizons, unearthing opportunities that were buried before. Our tech team at QXO built systems for customer-segment profiles and lead generation that are now helping our sales team secure new business. At XPO, internal tech stack modernization led to the creation of XPO Connect®, a customer-facing digital marketplace born from operational tools in the truckload industry. That technology is now a competitive offering of RXO, XPO's truckload spin-off.

Before I get into some technologies that deliver functional intelligence, a word of caution. When you're an acquirer, it's important to guard against any sense of superiority creeping into the integration process. It's not helpful to frame the tech transformation as fixing the crummy technology that the legacy company got wrong. It may be instinctive and come from a place of enthusiasm, but it sets up an "us versus them" mentality. A credible way to frame the tech changeover is as an exciting part of the integration that will deliver all kinds of good things for the new team members through collaboration. Strategically, this should take place in short order, but empathetically, understand that it comes at a time when the legacy employees already have a lot to deal with.

Demand Forecasting

This is the process by which a company predicts future demand for its products and services, as well as the likely timing of those purchases. It can also be used to predict price elasticity, which is essential for making informed pricing decisions. Given how many variables rely on demand forecasting, the predictions need to be accurate enough for management to make high-ticket decisions with confidence.

An integrated sales and operations planning process merges customer needs with SKU-level inventory data. It then incorporates information from the sales and marketing teams. The system utilizes predictive analytics to create demand forecasts that can look ahead from one week to 18 months, depending on how volatile the product is.

Once we've modeled the forecast, we calculate just enough safety stock to defend against surprises like a weather disaster, supply chain slowdown, or an unexpected spike in demand. Then we look across our network to see where we'll stand on inventory availability at that future time. Where are we short? Where are we heavy? Do we need to shift inventory or accelerate orders? Each day, we track actual demand against forecast, accounting for bias. If we're frequently overshooting or undershooting, we fix that.

Demand forecasting is a brilliant management tool, and it's also a self-improving, intelligent analytic, which is why it's an integration staple in our playbook. This may suit your company, or you may gravitate toward other kinds of predictive capabilities, depending on the industry and business model you choose.

Procurement

Procurement is a direct way to improve the profitability of the business. Every percentage point you cut from your spending translates to pure profit. My companies have spent billions of dollars annually on procurement, including product for resale, technology, transportation, real estate, travel, insurance, and equipment, and there are always ways to do better. If your company is looking for ways to double EBITDA, rationalizing procurement costs is a solid start.

After acquiring a business, our team often discovers that procurement practices are completely decentralized. We've even seen situations where over 1,000 employees in the field are making deals based on personal relationships. The same item from the same manufacturer might be bought by different branches at a 40% price swing. This gets rectified during the integration, when procurement transitions to a centralized model. But we still need to get a handle on the needs of the new branches to sort out the vendor relationships. We solve this by first mapping every product, category, price, and vendor; then we use AI analysis to find the anomalies. The spend gets ranked by SKU, category, and margin contribution, and we feed this data into forecasting models built by our procurement experts.

With the results in hand, our procurement team can buy smarter. And just as important, we're fixing inefficient behaviors that subtract from the bottom line. We tell vendors, "We're building something big here, and we want long-term partnerships, not just discounts. If you want to be a part of that, we need most-favored-nation pricing, improved terms, better allocations, and early notice on specials." It needs to be a two-way street, so in return, we'll share our forecasting to give the vendor a heads-up well before we need the product. This helps them run production more efficiently. We'll also commit to purchasing a set quantity of product well in advance and align our go-to-market strategies with those of key vendors to help them piggyback on our growth. Some vendors initially balk at these new relationship parameters, and that's okay. Others sign on and compete for our business on favorable terms.

When you have a centralized procurement process balanced with local insights, it shows up everywhere. You get a dollar-for-dollar improvement in EBITDA for every dollar in procurement savings, along with lower working capital, higher free cash flow, better pricing, and happier customers.

Inventory Management

Here's another reason why demand forecasting is nonnegotiable from my perspective: It's the crystal ball of rigorous inventory management. If you don't know what inventory you have, its location, and how fast it's selling, you're not practicing precision inventory management; you're just stockpiling.

> If you can't see your inventory in real time, you're not managing it; you're gambling with it.

My teams have done acquisitions where the inventory manager couldn't give us an accurate count of what we own. When that happens, we'll shut down the branch network for a weekend and do a full manual count. We've done that across hundreds of locations to get good baseline stock data before launching our inventory management system. This way, our data starts off on the right foot. We're simply not willing to inherit poor practices and bleed our margins.

Getting the inventory mix right is a big, big profit lever. To do this in a consistent, disciplined manner, we favor a real-time warehouse management system (WMS) capable of scanning every SKU on intake and tracking it through shelving, picking, and packing. The WMS maintains visibility of the item until it's outbound, at which point its record becomes part of the data lake. This, in turn, feeds the demand forecasting function. Accurate data improves everything, from customer service and labor productivity to utilization of warehouse space, and it eliminates the human error that comes from flying blind.

Transportation and Logistics

Not every company has core transportation operations, but there are some universal takeaways that relate to technology.

I'll share my experiences with full truckload, LTL, and local pickup-and-delivery operations. In each case, the goal is simple: Reduce the cost of transportation without sacrificing service quality. There's also a dotted line from transportation to logistics operations because the inventory being managed must be trucked inbound from the supplier to the warehouse and outbound to the customer.

The profitability of transportation operations stems from various factors, including route optimization, consolidating LTL freight into full truckloads, reducing fuel waste, utilizing owned fleet rather than third-party carriers, and planning for risk management. A transportation management system (TMS) is the backbone of these operations; it provides visibility into the availability of trucks and drivers, competitive bids, routing options, shipment tracking, and safety records. The days are gone when an efficient trucking operation could be run from a desk with a phone. With access to digital transportation networks, a TMS gets results that would be impossible to achieve manually.

XPO, which I led from 2011 to 2022, evolved into a pure-play transportation company. The field operators use an LTL-specific TMS platform to decide, on a case-by-case basis, whether to use XPO trucks and drivers or third-party carriers for long-haul freight. The analysis looks at cost, timing, equipment capacity, origin, destination, and risk. If the decision is to outsource the transportation, XPO can monitor the carrier's performance. If the decision is to insource, the software manages XPO's scheduling, maintenance, fuel usage, and safety. Either way, route optimization technology comes into play; this is a mainstay of transportation efficiency.

> Don't fall in love with your business model. Fall in love with what customers are willing to pay for.

A key commonality between transportation and logistics is that they're both network businesses with significant allocations of labor and assets. It's critical to understand what customers value most, because that's what they're willing to pay for. When integrating an acquisition, don't make an assumption that customers of the legacy business mirror your existing customers—they might have very different ideas of what stellar service looks like. For example, does an accelerated time frame from order to delivery matter more than price? This will affect how the WMS and TMS support fulfillment.

Customer expectations can also influence technology agendas, M&A decisions, real estate requirements, and staffing—essentially, large-scale allocations of resources. I always tell my teams to build the network for what it should look like, not what it happens to be today. My philosophy on scaling networks is industry-agnostic; it holds true whether the footprint is transportation terminals, equipment rental hubs, or distribution centers.

> Don't accept trade-offs between quality and speed. A world-class organization figures out how to do both.

Sometimes my teams and I have acquired mini-roll-up networks, where management bought a few businesses over the years but never optimized the operations. For example, a company may have six small distribution centers in a dense metropolitan market instead of one large efficient facility. We most often see this in companies coming out of private equity, where short ownership horizons discourage major investments in network redesign. For us, it's an opportunity for rapid improvement.

Pricing Optimization

Pricing is almost always the biggest profit opportunity in a business. There's no direct cost to price, so every extra penny you capture enhances your bottom line. But it's far from simple; I would wager that more mistakes are made with pricing than with any other business function. That's because guesswork is still alive and well, pricing is overly decentralized, or both. When pricing devolves into little or no cohesion between branches, that's a profit problem.

Price elasticity analysis is a much better way to go. This tool generates an estimate of how much volume will be gained or lost when a price is adjusted down or up. It uses predictive algorithms to inform decisions. At what price can you afford to lose 1% of volume and still come out ahead? How about 5% of volume? What increase in volume is necessary to offset a 2% decrease in price? That 2% reduction is coming right out of your margin percentage. And it gets more complex when you layer in seasonality, promotions, rebates, distance to destination, cross-price effects, market segmentation, product life cycles, and brand perception.

I place a high value on assembling a pricing team that seats super-sharp mathematicians alongside seasoned pricing pros. We look for people from industries where dynamic pricing is the bedrock of transactions, such as trucking, airlines, and hotels. They've mastered elasticity, and they understand demand curves, seasonality, regional behavior, and supply constraints—the whole equation. That doesn't mean we ignore pricing talent inside our own industry, but we're also looking for that fresh set of eyes.

Over the years, we've developed a tool kit of intelligent pricing mechanisms that understand various operations. For example, we have algorithmic pricing plugged into our ERP. This sets a minimum sell price on products and services, and the more a salesperson sells above it, the bigger the commission. Going below that minimum requires preapproval and a strong justification. We can also match pricing to inventory quantity, taking forecasted demand into account. It's driven entirely by data.

Given the importance of pricing discipline, I believe that a pricing KPI should be tied directly to sales compensation. A salesperson who routinely drags prices to the floor—and with that, gross margin—learns there's no reward in that behavior. It's also not fun to watch the person next to you make a lot of money—and with our dashboard, everyone can see that in real time. We've developed a color-coded stack ranking of salespeople that tells the story at one glance. No one wants to be at the bottom of the stack.

Importantly, pricing will never be a one-time exercise.

We continually recalibrate, test, reanalyze, and adjust pricing bands. The more data the models ingest, the sharper they get. But success also depends on the field's buy-in of the corporate pricing strategy. The model must work in practice, with compensation that rewards salespeople with substantial bonuses for driving price, volume, and profit. That buy-in creates a powerful alliance between the pricing team and the sales force because then everyone agrees on the metrics that define winning.

Sales Force Effectiveness

I've heard executives say that onboarding legacy salespeople is one of the more challenging aspects of an acquisition, and I don't disagree. It's certainly multifaceted—an integration of strong personalities, industry relationships, culture, compensation, and organizational structure.

Many companies I've bought came with strong sales talent, but the sales organization itself was not rigorously aligned with the growth strategy. In some cases, the salespeople weren't adequately trained, or they didn't understand the tech well enough to realize its potential. Others chose to rely too much on personal relationships and too little on data. That's just the norm for salespeople in a lot of sectors.

A comprehensive lead-generation engine is a cornerstone of our integration playbook, and we move forward quickly to help the team sign new customers and grow our addressable market. It's a combination of CRM analytics, public data, internal data, and AI insights. Who aren't we reaching that we should be selling to? Is our definition of the addressable market too limiting? Which customers are within reach of our footprint but buying from our competitors instead? We want to grow our profit at a much faster rate than market growth, and that requires growing our book of business.

> **A customer relationship is like any other relationship. To succeed, both sides need to show how much they value it and be willing to change to improve it.**

The next technical piece, the CRM, is a sales team's collective memory. It's where every customer interaction—calls, emails, quotes, transactional wins and losses—gets documented and logged for relationship management. We standardize on a single CRM platform across the company, and we require full compliance. If it's not in the CRM, it didn't happen. A big chunk of our sales training focuses on the importance of knowing who we're calling on, what we're quoting, and how many touches it took to close a deal. Without that knowledge, we can't improve, benchmark, or replicate success—and we don't pay commissions on transactions that aren't fully documented in the system.

> Pay people generously, but only for exceptional performance.

The sales commission structure is one of the most effective levers for profitable growth; it's a critical point of alignment between performance and compensation. The structure should be crystal clear to every salesperson: Meet your numbers, and you get paid; exceed them, and you get paid more. I don't like to cap sales bonuses because it goes against human nature. Even self-motivated people check out to some degree when they hit their cap. I much prefer incentive programs that create enlightened self-interest, where a result that benefits the company also benefits individuals and their families. We give them a clear path to do that effectively.

Another sales tool I highly recommend is what we call the "win room," which is a virtual sales lab. Leaders from sales, marketing, and operations collaborate in the win room to test, tweak, and scale new ideas. This is where we pressure-test new lead sources for accuracy, run pilot programs in targeted regions, and decide what's ready for national roll-out. It's also where we surface and disseminate best practices, analyze the profitability of strategies like private labeling, and build campaigns around high-margin offerings.

In short, we use our technology to harmonize the sales organization, analyze data to find the gaps in our market outreach, and incentivize our salespeople to close them. It's a widely applicable approach. Our tactical use of technology at XPO was instrumental in doubling the profits of the legacy Con-way and Norbert Dentressangle operations. Both companies were respected leaders in their fields, yet we were still able to improve their operations as part of XPO.

E-Commerce

Some businesses claim to offer e-commerce when it's really a glorified catalog with a checkout button. There's not much value to be gained from that. When exploring a potential acquisition that says they have e-commerce, the first question we ask is, "Is your platform truly self-service, end to end, with no human intervention?" If the answer is no, it's just an e-order submission. The customer clicks a button, someone in the back office gets an email and manually keys the order in, and someone else tracks down the stock. That system doesn't scale. By contrast, a truly integrated, zero-touch e-commerce platform is a scalable extension of the sales engine.

Real e-commerce starts with a front-end user interface that's fast and intuitive, and it connects to a robust back end. Inventory management, pricing, order fulfillment, communication, transportation, transactional processes, and customer history are all automated, as is search functionality. Best-in-class search functions are designed with intelligent synonyms, autocompletion, filters, and customer line of sight to availability. The WMS facilitates access to the product, and the TMS tracks the transit. Demand forecasting ingests the order data for inventory management analysis.

Once an e-commerce platform is live, it becomes a powerful source of insights—and what a customer fails to buy can be as important as the purchase. Where did the customer go when browsing? What SKUs were added to the cart but not bought? What are the sales conversion rates by geography, time of day, and customer segment? This data can be used to support pricing decisions, stocking strategies, cross-sell opportunities, and a personalized online experience that drives revenue.

Financial Planning and Analysis

While not an operational department, the financial planning and analysis (FP&A) group is worth mentioning because this group's work informs all capital allocation decisions, including M&A. One or more FP&A experts should be deeply embedded in the process of transforming an acquired company. This is when ideas are flying around like crazy and need to be quantified into expectations.

The operations integration team might say, "We've got 10 initiatives we believe will create alpha for shareholders." From there, FP&A assigns probabilities of success—initiatives that rate 90% are essentially in the bag. Others may be long shots at 10% or 20% but have a high upside if they succeed. Long shots like these are worth discussing, even if the plan gives them minimal credit.

Good FP&A leaders can quickly spot sandbagging and overpromising. They ensure that the transformation process moves forward in a systematic way. Beyond M&A, FP&A aligns the budget with strategy, adjusting for changes in operations and capital resources. They make sure every dollar spent is backed by a thorough analysis. When a company leverages its FP&A talent as a strategic asset and not merely as number crunchers, leadership can move fast and deliver more consistent results for shareholders.

> **Extraordinary shareholder value creation can only happen if customers are ecstatic about the quality of your service.**

None of these operational successes occur in isolation. A fully integrated tech stack transforms your business into one holistic organism, where every function operates in sync with speed and discipline and returns from M&A are compounded. Integration goes beyond efficiency; it creates a scalable platform that delivers value long after the deal closes.

The Ultimate Opportunity

TWO RECURRING THEMES APPEAR throughout this book: the importance of context in both life and business and the significance of big trends in achieving large-scale success. The biggest trend of all is technology.

The history of technology chronicles the development of tools, systems, and processes to solve human needs. We humans have used our three-pound blob of brain jelly to devise ways to outsource our senses, memory, emotions, environmental interactions, and virtually every aspect of daily life. We've shown a determination to survive in increasingly sophisticated ways, from the creation of early stone tools to AI—and it's this continuum of innovation that makes our lives more efficient and comfortable.

Over the past two million years, human inventiveness has traced an exponential curve: initially slow, then accelerating in velocity. Early milestones, such as implements for hunting and control of fire, unfolded gradually, empowering humans to survive and reproduce in dangerous environments. Each incremental invention has paved the way for more complex tools and technologies, with the intervals shrinking between major breakthroughs. Today, the swift rise of genomics, robotics, AI, and nanotechnology perpetuates this trend, condensing the pace of advancement from centuries to years—and even months.

A New Paradigm

Darwinian evolution occurs through sexual reproduction, where genes that confer traits better suited to the environment become increasingly prevalent within a species. Over many generations of adaptation, advantageous traits accumulate to the point of giving rise to new species. This is the context of human evolution as we know it today, but is it the big trend? Things may be changing.

I envision a future where evolution of the human species

transitions from the current carbon-based model to a silicon-based model powered by AI, as Ray Kurzweil does. In this new paradigm, our ongoing adaptation no longer depends solely on the trial-and-error mutations of our DNA. Instead, it would be guided by the merging of natural selection and "unnatural selection"—a process driven by invented technologies, geopolitical objectives, and market dynamics. This model would accelerate human evolution to match the rapid pace of innovation, but it brings both considerable peril and the immense potential to create a utopia.

To put this in perspective, consider that 332 years elapsed between Galileo looking at the stars through his telescope and the James Webb Space Telescope producing an image of a galaxy cluster four billion light-years from Earth. But it took only 12 years to move from IBM's development of AI that understands human language to Google's revolutionary AI modeling of more than 200 million protein structures—now being used in research ranging from drug therapies to biofuels. The Timeline of Unnatural Selection in Appendix 2 shows that the pace of innovation throughout history has increased and is accelerating.

The unprecedented speed and scope of today's technological change are being fueled by vast data networks, the explosive growth of computational power, and human ingenuity. Thinking through where all this might be headed, I can envision four possible scenarios for humankind's future state. The first two are grim, but the latter two are profoundly beautiful.

> **What we do with AI will shape not just what we become, but whether we survive to become anything at all.**

Potential Future States

Scenario 1. AI inherits the darker aspects of human nature—our intolerance, biases, and aggression—and ultimately turns against us, exterminating our species. I assess the probability of Scenario 1 at 10%.

Scenario 2. This would be equally as catastrophic as Scenario 1. The threat in this scenario stems not from AI itself but from authoritarian regimes or terrorists wielding AI as a tool for mass annihilation. I assign Scenario 2 a 25% probability.

Scenarios 3 and 4. Far more hopefully, I can envision a future where we humans harness advanced technologies to build a global utopian society, achieve peace, eliminate poverty and famine, and live long and healthy lives devoted to meaningful pursuits. A future where resources are abundant and available to everyone. The difference between these two outcomes is that in Scenario 3, we achieve utopia while retaining our distinct identity as *Homo sapiens*, separate from our technological creations. In Scenario 4, humans merge with technology so intricately that we evolve into an advanced superspecies sharing the same structure. I assign a 35% probability to Scenario 3 and 30% to Scenario 4.

> **Human extinction might not come from war but from a transformation into an unrecognizably different species.**

Scenario 1: AI Could Wipe Out the Human Race

AI, designed by humans and trained on vast datasets of our history, could inherit humanity's darker impulses, including violence and murder. By modeling AI on human thought patterns, we risk transmitting our destructive traits into entities far more intelligent and powerful than ourselves. An AI system that analyzes human history might logically conclude that domination, violence, or even genocide represent viable solutions to certain objectives, replicating our failings on a terrifying scale.

This risk arises because AI technology is intended to reflect human tendencies, similar to the theological principle that humanity is created in the image of the divine. The large language models of AI are constantly learning by consuming what humans upload to the internet—everything from Wikipedia entries and Reddit posts to personal blog archives and online news articles, scraping billions of pieces of text, audio, code, and visual material to build statistical approximations of human thinking.

Humans are great at many things—and vastly superior to other members of the animal kingdom in most ways. But we're quite flawed in one important way: It's rare for members of the same species to kill each other en masse until it comes to humans.

Humans kill each other in large numbers for irrational, political, economic, and religious reasons. This is because evolution has equipped us with deep-rooted survival instincts inherited from our hunter-gatherer ancestors, including aggressive competition for resources such as food, shelter, and mates, as well as traits such as territorial defense and tribalism. These traits once provided protection in hostile environments; now they manifest as useless, destructive behaviors.

Evolution plays out gradually over many generations, so we're perpetually "dancing with the ghosts of our ancestors." Some traits that enabled survival tens of thousands of years ago are especially maladaptive today, surfacing in ways that cause harm, like war, gang violence, and divisive mindsets—a result of tribalism. Humans evolved as social beings reliant on tight-knit groups for survival, creating an inherent tendency to favor those within the group. Today, this shows up in behaviors such as nationalism, racism, and ideological polarization, often leading to violence toward perceived outsiders.

These flaws highlight how intensely humans can fail to get along with each other. Look at ants and bees (and plenty of other species); they're much better than we are at cooperation. They form superorganisms—functioning groups composed of individual organisms, each with a specialized role that benefits the whole. Humans are far from a superorganism: 25% of our species lack access to clean water, nearly 10% go to bed hungry each night, and the majority of global deaths are considered preventable. We have access to enormous resources, but we're just not good at cooperating with each other on a large scale. In fact, we're not good at sharing in general. We revert to tribalism, thinking in petty ways, holding rigidly to our beliefs, and being intolerant of those with different beliefs.

While the AI we're creating doesn't share our biological DNA, it reflects our innate tendencies; this could lead to violence on a grand scale. In short, humanity could face an existential threat born of our own creation: AI that turns our most destructive impulses back on us, resulting in our extinction.

If the technology perceives humanity as an inherent obstacle to achieving worthy objectives, it might logically decide that our extermination is necessary. An advanced AI system could orchestrate humanity's downfall without any human participation through any of the following ways:

- Creating biotechnological disasters or exploiting genetic engineering or synthetic biology to unleash unstoppable super pathogens.

- Interfering with large geoengineering projects designed to combat climate change, or interfering with the environment in disruptive ways to make the planet uninhabitable for humans. Examples of interference could be reflecting sunlight away from Earth, altering the atmosphere to create extreme weather patterns, or triggering earthquakes with targeted detonations at fault lines.

- Paralyzing populations remotely by seizing control of digital infrastructure, such as power grids, water treatment plants, air traffic control systems, and national communication networks.

- Taking control of military systems to deploy autonomous drones, combat-ready robots, and missile systems against civilians or strategic sites, bypassing human command chains.

- Crippling the financial markets to crash global economies and trigger devastating shortages of resources.

- Weaponizing developments in nanotechnology—such as self-replicating nanobots, which could potentially consume all biomass in a Drexler "gray goo" scenario.

- Provoking civil wars, genocides, or widespread despair by turning members of society against each other through misinformation campaigns, deepfakes, and social media manipulation.

The tragedy would lie not only in our extinction but also in the realization that the seeds of our downfall were planted by our encoded weaknesses. Instead of ushering in an era of prosperity, Scenario 1 would be the ultimate irony: humanity undone by technology created by us and in our own image.

> The greatest risk of building technology in our own image is that we humans have serious imperfections.

Scenario 2: AI Might Enable Asymmetric Annihilation

Alternatively, AI itself doesn't decide to kill us but is weaponized by bad actors as a tool for mass annihilation. All the same possibilities listed under Scenario 1 apply here. The asymmetry would come from a huge gap in capability. AI could give one nation-state overwhelming dominance, using surveillance, cyber warfare, and autonomous weapons to eliminate a weaker rival's infrastructure, economy, or population. And it could happen quickly, with AI magnifying a small imbalance between nation-states to create a chasm, leaving the target with no meaningful defense.

This differs from the current world order, where mutually assured destruction acts as a nuclear deterrent: The first one who pushes the button commits not just homicide but suicide. Under Scenario 2, though, countries like China, North

Korea, or Russia might be tempted to deploy AI-based weapons in a bid for global dominance. As long as one party has the capacity to destroy another without fear of retribution, the threat is out of balance. And it's not entirely inconceivable that even a freedom-loving, democratic nation like the United States could, under some future political landscape, find itself tempted to misuse AI in ways that undermine those very values.

Of particular concern would be AI's ability to put targeted bioweapons—such as viruses engineered to harm populations with a specific ethnicity, genetic marker, or geographic presence—into the hands of authoritarian regimes. Unlike traditional bioweapons, these viruses could be designed to spread quietly and selectively, delaying detection until the impact becomes irreversible. Equally as concerning is the idea of large powerful nation-states as targets. When technology gives players with few resources—small nation-states or terrorists—the ability to strike major powers without direct engagement, traditional deterrence mechanisms are bypassed.

Ironically, these mass disasters would be enabled by innovations originally intended to elevate the human condition. They would become modern analogs to nuclear devastation, permanently altering the geopolitical landscape.

Scenario 3: Utopia!

In this scenario, humanity's noblest aspirations—longevity, health, happiness, harmony, peace, and love—are amplified to extraordinary heights. Technology is harnessed for constructive purposes, eradicating poverty, illness, crime, and conflict on a global scale. This ushers in an era of human relationships that are deeply enriched and collaborative. Our understanding of the universe deepens, the arts flourish, and civilization advances to new heights.

> Technology has the potential to eradicate poverty, disease, and conflict, enabling global peace, longevity, and happiness.

It would take a societal reset of great magnitude to realize Scenario 3 as I envision it—but humans are well versed in triumphing through evolutionary change. I believe that we're already on a path that could lead to a state of utopia. If so, artists, musicians, and storytellers someday will create rich cultural works that memorialize the Great Transformation and the liberation of our species to realize our full potential.

The Great Transformation

Just as I outlined in Chapters 5, 6, and 7 on business transformation, it's ultimately execution that matters. AI excels at that. Sit back with me and soak up the many things that *could* be possible in terms of creating a universally happy, healthy, peaceful world where humanity is empowered to solve global challenges.

> Technology can amplify humanity's noblest aspirations—harmony, peace, and love—to extraordinary heights.

Under Scenario 3, as technology advances, military and other governmental structures will dissolve. Tax systems will fade away alongside global monetary systems. The institutions we currently rely on will be transformed by global intelligence systems. Public services will be managed with unparalleled efficiency; for example, traditional education systems will be replaced by experiential knowledge delivered through direct neural stimulation. Human health will undergo a complete transformation through AI, with cancer, heart disease, dementia, and other illnesses eradicated, and with both physical and mental vitality enduring well into advanced age.

Economically, the Great Transformation will be defined by massive deflation, with the cost of goods and services declining to near zero through superefficient supply chains. Money will become a curious artifact, as humans will no longer have any use for it. If this sounds impossible, consider that the idea of trading shells or coins for goods has only been a part of human history for a few thousand years—a nanosecond in terms of our existence. Before that, humans had no concept of needing to make more and more money to buy more and more stuff.

Here are some additional aspects of future life that could be intrinsically elevated by AI:

- Advanced renewable energy systems, including solar, wind, and fusion, will provide clean, limitless energy. Carbon emissions will be reduced to net zero.

- Clean water will be universally accessible through AI-managed desalination technologies and ocean cleanup operations.

- AI-managed reforestation and other habitat protections will reverse environmental degradation and restore biodiversity.

- Geoengineering and carbon capture technologies will reverse climate change and stabilize global ecosystems.

- AI-precision farming, vertical agriculture, and lab-grown proteins will produce nutritious food in abundance, ending hunger.

- 3D printing, modular construction, and automated production will deliver eco-friendly homes at low cost, eliminating housing shortages.

- Advanced robotics and AI-managed factories will produce goods efficiently and at near-zero cost, ensuring universal access to clothing, tools, and household items.

- Nanobots and AI diagnostics will detect diseases before they manifest as symptoms, facilitating early intervention and treatments.

- AI will accelerate the development of personalized drugs, vaccines, and regenerative therapies that can cure or halt most illnesses and make pandemics obsolete.

- Gene editing, nanomedicine, and cellular repair technologies will slow or even reverse biological aging, greatly extending healthy lifespans.

- Implanted technologies and therapies will restore sight, hearing, speech, and mobility, removing long-standing physical limitations.

- AI therapists and brain–computer interfaces will provide perpetual access to stigma-free support for managing anxiety, depression, and personality disorders.

- Neural implants will connect human minds to an AI-curated universal knowledge base of all subjects and skills. This will expand human intelligence, memory, and creativity far beyond our current capabilities.

- Communities will feature smart infrastructure for recycling and upcycling, resulting in near-total materials reuse and eliminating waste and mitigating the drain on natural resources.

- Transportation will be powered by clean energy and autonomous systems, such as hyperloop networks and flying vehicles. This will reduce congestion and pollution.

- AI-based supply chains will coordinate the distribution of food, water, shelter, and healthcare, ensuring that every person's essential needs are met.

- AI will facilitate conflict resolution, using predictive algorithms to mediate disputes before they escalate by modeling cultural, economic, and historical data. This will foster peace on global and local levels.

- Language barriers will be eliminated as AI cultural mediators dismantle barriers to global empathy and cooperation.

- Virtual reality will enable people to experience the perspectives of others, dissipating prejudice.

To facilitate the Great Transformation, autonomous robots will serve as central agents of personal and societal support. For society, they will supply the minimal labor needed for the common good, with most work being subsumed by AI. This will reduce human work hours to zero. For individuals, companion robots will function as personal assistants, household staff, mentors, therapists, creative collaborators, diplomatic mediators, and friends. Designed with a humanlike appearance, voice, and behaviors, each robot will be customized with the personality and aesthetics preferred by its human.

Humanoid robots will also improve mental health by providing empathetic support—responding to emotional cues and engaging constructively across various interactions. Incapable of thinking illogically themselves, they will help identify irrational beliefs and cognitive distortions to enhance psychological stability. For elderly, isolated, or emotionally strained people, a lifelike presence can represent trusted companionship. Some individuals and robots will develop nurturing long-term relationships.

Scenario 4: Beyond Utopia

This scenario envisions humankind reaping the benefits of Scenario 3 but going even further. The arrival of the Singularity, as Ray Kurzweil foresees it, becomes a story of near-infinite human potential. Kurzweil believes that humans and technology will blend so seamlessly that we'll transcend our old limitations, evolving into a new form of life that carries the best of what we are into an even more extraordinary future.[1]

If we merge with AI through technologies like brain–computer interfaces, we'll be opening a new chapter filled with limitless possibilities. The distinction between human and machine will dissolve, erasing the boundary that once separated the organic from the artificial. Human creativity, curiosity, and wisdom will be amplified, allowing us to explore new realms of experience and understanding. Our legacy doesn't vanish; it evolves.

In this bright vision, our species transforms but retains some of our human essence, such as core values and aspirations for ourselves and others. We become pioneers in a new epoch defined not by biology but by technology, and with a deeper understanding of existence across the cosmos. The best of the human spirit endures as the fragile human brain gives way to new, more durable and adaptive forms of consciousness—synthetic intelligence and postbiological minds.

> The boundary between human and machine might blur, with our consciousness existing as pure information.

This transformation may seem improbable, yet it follows a profound evolutionary logic. While roughly 8.7 million species inhabit the Earth today, they represent less than 1% of all species that ever existed; more than 99% have gone extinct. It's not unthinkable that humanity, too, might yield to something greater. However, unlike past Darwinian extinctions, this is not a vanishing but a becoming. Our consciousness, once confined to the brain, may come to exist as pure information, inhabiting digital networks, planetary ecologies, or interstellar domains. Rather than being replaced by superior entities, we become them. Rather than perishing, we transcend.

Think of Scenario 4 as humanity's greatest adventure—where our essence continues in astonishing new forms, bringing intelligence and meaning to a future unbounded by even the stars.

Who Wants to Be a Billionaire?

You might be asking yourself, *Isn't it strange to end a book about making a few billion dollars by talking about a future where presumably no billionaires exist?* I don't see it that way. I think that if we were to achieve Scenario 3 or 4, everyone could live like a billionaire.

Think about it: What does that really mean—to live like a billionaire?

Today, it means having wealth you can use to improve life as you see fit, such as choosing to use your wealth to improve your health and the health of people you care about, to extend your life and theirs, and to do whatever you want with your time. You may choose to provide these same things for people you don't know but who are in need.

> In the future, everyone could have resources surpassing today's wealthiest individuals, enabling long, healthy, and fulfilling lives.

Now think of the wealthiest people in the world today and everything they can do with their money. That's just a small fraction of how well everyone could live in a utopia that fully harnesses technology. If our model of humanity is turned upside down, every person would have more inherent capability, more influence over their life, and a far more enjoyable life than the richest person alive today. In fact, the entire concept of rich versus poor would be obsolete. I believe this is possible if we use AI and other technologies wisely.

That, in the end, is my utopian vision. It's clear that Scenarios 3 and 4 are a whole lot better than the darker paths of 1 and 2. So, let's resolve to avoid the tragedies of the first two scenarios and commit to doing everything in our power to steer our future toward the much brighter outcomes.

One final and critical observation: Throughout my career building multibillion-dollar public companies— United Waste Systems, United Rentals, XPO, GXO, RXO, and QXO—I've learned that the greatest success comes from proactively embracing change. We have to respect the enormous potential of AI, understand its risks instead of blindly fearing them, and use it strategically to our advantage.

> We stand at the edge of the ultimate entrepreneurial opportunity, where we can proactively shape the future of our species.

The moment we're in *right now* is the ultimate entrepreneurial opportunity. The choices we make *today* will echo through generations, potentially determining whether humanity flourishes or fails. I encourage you to actively engage with these powerful technologies to master them. By consciously directing our innovations toward outcomes that uplift humanity—that reflect our best intentions and most magical dreams—we can ensure that the future we get is the future we want.

When we look back years from now, I hope we'll see this era as a pivotal chapter for our global society—one in which human ingenuity triumphs not by chance but by choice.

Summary of Book One: How to Make a Few Billion Dollars (2023)

HERE'S A SYNOPSIS OF the key points from my first book, *How to Make a Few Billion Dollars,* published in 2023. In it, I share insights into replicating success by reflecting on my own blunders and triumphs.

Introduction

- As of 2023, I had led seven billion-dollar or multi-billion-dollar companies, completed approximately

500 acquisitions, and opened more than 250 green-field locations. In 2024, I started my eighth enterprise, QXO, which became a multibillion-dollar company in 10 months.

- I discuss why I respect public equity markets as a way of validating success through free-market economics. The markets also facilitate capital raising, vibrant corporate cultures, and large-scale brand building.

- The book is essentially a guide for wealth creation and achieving big goals in various aspects of life. I draw from my experience throughout my career, summarized here as company milestones. My leadership spans are shown in parentheses.

  » I started Amerex Oil Associates (1979–1983) at age 23 with minimal experience and grew the company to $4.7 billion in annual brokerage volume, in part by arbitraging between cash and futures markets.

  » I started Hamilton Resources (1984–1989) in London, generating $1 billion annually through opportunistic, complex oil trading.

» I founded United Waste Systems (1989–1997) as my first public company, built it into the fifth-largest solid waste management company in the United States, and sold it for $2.5 billion, outperforming the S&P 500 by 5.6x.

» I founded United Rentals (1997–2007) and led it to become the world's largest construction equipment rental company in 13 months, with a "100-bagger" stock by the end of its first decade. Subsequently, the stock became a "200-bagger," meaning the share price at inception was $3.50 and its stock rose to over 200x that price.

» I built XPO (2011–present) into a global transportation and logistics leader, growing its stock to a "32-bagger" that ranked as the seventh-best-performing Fortune 500 stock of the last decade. XPO stock has subsequently become a "50-bagger."

» As XPO entered its second decade, my team and I executed a successful value-creation strategy by spinning off GXO Logistics (2021–present) and RXO from XPO, creating three separate public companies.

Chapter 1: How to Rearrange Your Brain

- Truly smart people are humble and remain open to continual learning from others. Genuine intelligence involves recognizing that one's own knowledge is limited and can be improved by other perspectives. Cultivating this mindset fosters both personal growth and effective collaboration.

- Achieving ambitious goals requires thinking differently—sometimes very differently. Conventional thinking can restrict creativity and limit your potential. Adopting unconventional thought processes and challenging traditional views can dramatically enhance your ability to accomplish significant objectives.

- *Gedankenexperiments* (thought experiments involving vivid, intentional daydreaming) are powerful mental exercises that spark creativity and expansive thinking. By engaging your imagination and envisioning hypothetical scenarios, you can explore possibilities beyond your current understanding. These mental practices encourage innovative problem-solving and broader perspectives.

- Cultivating a "love vibe" within a business environment can effectively neutralize conflicts and improve decision-making. Approaching workplace relationships and challenges with genuine empathy and positive emotional engagement can diffuse tension, creating a collaborative, productive atmosphere.

- At my eldest daughter's wedding, I guided the guests through a unique thought experiment designed to project universal love toward the bride and groom. By imagining all instances of human love from the past, present, and future, we collectively channeled positive emotions, creating an expansive feeling of unity. For me, this underscored how cultivating a love vibe can significantly enhance interactions.

- "Gratitude conversations" among colleagues foster positive emotions and reinforce constructive workplace relationships. By actively expressing sincere appreciation, you can strengthen bonds within teams, build morale, and create a harmonious work environment.

- You can encourage positive outcomes by reframing negative thoughts as exaggerated survival mechanisms inherited from our evolutionary ancestors. When you understand that automatic negative thoughts typically stem from overstated fears, you can maintain a more optimistic, resilient outlook in the face of challenges.

- It's essential to accept personal imperfections and acknowledge that mistakes are inevitable when striving for ambitious goals. Embracing the reality of occasional goof-ups fosters emotional resilience, encourages ongoing effort, and supports progress toward significant achievements.

- By embracing problems as valuable opportunities, you can transform them into pathways for achieving success. This shift in perspective helps maintain motivation and fosters proactive problem-solving.

- You can avoid rigid thought patterns by embracing dialectical thinking, which acknowledges multiple valid perspectives. By recognizing personal imperfections and acting without waiting for perfect conditions, you'll become a more effective leader, especially in uncertain circumstances.

- Practicing radical acceptance means fully accepting reality as it is—relinquishing the illusion of control. By adopting this approach, you can make logical, forward-looking decisions unclouded by wishful thinking or frustration with uncontrollable factors.

• Focusing attention nonjudgmentally in a work environment enhances efficiency and objectivity. Suspending judgment helps eliminate biases, reduces stress, and allows for clearer, more productive engagement with tasks and team interactions.

• Setting specific, ambitious goals that initially seem unattainable can drive you to achieve extraordinary things. Aspire to "think huge," and you'll expand your vision, motivating yourself to go beyond your perceived limitations.

• Clarity comes from staying humble and avoiding feelings of invincibility. By continuously seeking new knowledge and maintaining awareness of your small role in the vast universe, your self-perception will lead to more personal and professional growth.

• Inspired by psychologist Martin Seligman, I changed the way I interacted with my children by asking them each evening, "What was the happiest moment of your day?" rather than "How was your day?" This small adjustment dramatically shifted their perspective, training them to seek and expect positivity daily. It taught me the power of reframing experiences and the impact this has on our emotional outlook and mental well-being.

- In 2007, I stepped down as CEO of United Rentals so I could plan my next big thing. Instead, I encountered a period of intense depression and disorientation filled with uncertainty about my purpose in life. Seeking help, I delved deeply into cognitive behavioral therapy (CBT), where I learned to manage my cognitive distortions, such as catastrophizing, perfectionism, and dichotomous thinking. When I notice I'm feeling anxious about something, I ask myself a basic CBT question: *What's the worst that could happen, and how would I cope with that?* or *If a friend had a similar worry, how would I advise them to handle it?*

- I have a bronze sculpture on my property titled *Large, Sad Sphere* by artist Tom Otterness; it depicts a humanoid figure slouched in sadness with a box on top of its head. This sculpture symbolizes, for me, the limitations imposed by "thinking inside a box." It continually reminds me to think expansively, avoiding self-imposed constraints that limit creative solutions.

- Inside my home, I have Lincoln Schatz's dynamic art installation *Cluster*, which juxtaposes video clips of family and friends from various points in time. Observing this stimulates my brain to think fluidly about time and space, effectively rearranging my mental approach to problem-solving. It helps me detach from immediate concerns and view challenges from a broader, more creative perspective.

- I'm inspired by the way Albert Einstein used *gedanken-experiments* to creatively solve complex problems. I regularly use this method myself, visualizing large concepts such as the universe's evolution or the vastness of space and time, which I believe expands my cognitive capabilities. These experiments help me come up with novel solutions in both professional and personal situations.

- Meditation has been my primary hobby since my teenage years and has profoundly influenced me. Through consistent meditation practice, I achieve a state of deep calm, clarity, and creativity, enhancing my ability to handle challenges. This discipline has become essential in maintaining my focus and emotional resilience, especially during periods of intense business pressure.

- Ludwig Jesselson was the CEO of Philipp Brothers in the mid-20th century. "Phibro" was the world's largest commodity trading firm at the time, dominant in metals, minerals, and oil. Mr. Jesselson was an important mentor of mine, fundamentally shaping my business philosophy by teaching me that problems should be embraced as valuable opportunities. He demonstrated that viewing business challenges as assets rather than setbacks opens the door to innovation and competitive advantages. Adopting his perspective allowed me to solve complex problems proactively, creating significant value in my ventures.

- Another CEO taught me the concept of the M&A "bingo quadrant," which categorizes deals based on size and risk. In one quadrant, there are big, flawless deals, which unfortunately don't exist. Another quadrant has small, hairy deals, which are the worst. The third quadrant has small, good deals, whose smallness prevents you from creating big alpha. The fourth quadrant, known as "big, hairy deals with solvable problems," represents the greatest potential for high returns. Embracing complex opportunities and learning to overcome their inherent challenges has been instrumental to my success in M&A.

- While running United Rentals, I faced a significant financial setback—a $500 million loss due to miscalculations regarding anticipated government funding from the Transportation Equity Act (TEA-21). By applying radical acceptance, I confronted the loss honestly rather than compounding the error with denial and poor decisions. By accepting the reality, I was able to move forward strategically, turning this experience into an enduring lesson on managing downside scenarios.

- In 2007, United Rentals had an agreement to be acquired by Cerberus Capital Management when Cerberus unexpectedly defaulted on the deal amid the Great Financial Crisis, causing a 31% plunge in United stock. Although intensely challenging, we persevered, recovering strongly to become a top-performing stock.

- In 2018, XPO faced a severe short-seller attack, resulting in an immediate 26% stock price drop. Instead of panicking, my team applied radical acceptance and maintained frequent communication, both internally and externally. We decisively executed a $2 billion stock buyback—a move deemed risky by advisors at the time—which ultimately yielded a $4 billion profit after the stock rebounded strongly. This demonstrated how staying calm in a crisis can lead to substantial value creation.

- My college music teacher, the renowned jazz musician Bill Dixon, once confronted me about my pursuit of wealth, bluntly stating that I was "wasting my life" by chasing money instead of dedicating myself to music. Although painful, this critique deeply influenced my perspective. Bill was emphasizing the importance of societal impact and personal fulfillment beyond financial success. His honest feedback has stayed with me as a reminder to maintain a balanced perspective in life and pursue goals that have genuine meaning.

Chapter 2: How to Get the Major Trend Right

- You can make numerous mistakes in business and still succeed if you accurately align with the dominant industry trend. Technology is the current overarching megatrend, and its evolution is accelerating significantly. Businesses that ignore this megatrend are likely to face severe challenges or collapse.

- To thoroughly analyze an industry, it's essential to absorb all available information. This involves extensive research across multiple sources, from trade journals to analyst reports, to gain a comprehensive understanding of the industry.

- I target industries characterized by high scalability, rapid growth, substantial economies of scale, and ample opportunities for M&A. These factors are the cornerstones of a company's ability to create outsized shareholder value. Industries with these characteristics represent the greatest potential for long-term growth and profitability.

- A robust investment in technology is critical to success in nearly every industry today. Technology not only generates operational efficiencies; it also offers significant competitive advantages. Businesses that invest wisely in technology position themselves to capitalize on evolving market opportunities.

- An effective research approach consists of three stages: first, extensive self-education about the industry; second, the compilation of critical questions that need addressing; and third, in-depth interviews with the most knowledgeable industry experts. This structured methodology ensures a deep understanding of the industry backdrop and mitigates risk. It also aids in making informed decisions that drive long-term value.

- AI is rapidly becoming the key transformative technology of the future, with the power to disrupt existing industries and simultaneously create immense opportunities. To avoid obsolescence, business leaders must be proactive in considering how AI will reshape their sectors. AI's impact is inevitable across nearly all industries; the risk lies in not harnessing its potential.

- A company can develop a powerful innovation agenda by gathering insights from customers, employees, and vendors regarding their ideal technological solutions. Soliciting "dream tech" ideas from stakeholders helps a business anticipate market demand, whereas proactive dialogue often leads to practical and profitable developments.

- It's important to monitor disruptive technologies, such as 3D printing (industrial additive manufacturing) and intelligent automation, given their potential to fundamentally reshape supply chains and geopolitical dynamics. Understanding the long-term implications of technology and integrating this understanding into strategic planning can position a company ahead of competitors and help it maintain relevance.

- The logistics sector is swiftly advancing toward increased automation, making operations more efficient and cost-effective. Automation significantly reduces manual labor requirements, enhances accuracy, and boosts overall productivity. Logistics companies must be proactive in adopting automation to maintain industry competitiveness.

- History illustrates the danger of failing to remain vigilant about major technological trends; examples include Thomas Watson of IBM dismissing the future of computers and Clifford Stoll of *Newsweek* underestimating the internet. These cautionary tales underscore the critical importance of accurately forecasting tech developments.

- The book *The Singularity Is Near*, by Ray Kurzweil, continues to have a major influence on forward-looking thinking on technology, particularly in its discussion of the rapid convergence of humans and machines. It outlines how technological growth will eventually surpass human capability, creating unprecedented opportunities and challenges. Contemplation of visionary insights like the Singularity helps with strategic planning and trend anticipation.

- AI's powerfully disruptive potential was a factor throughout my analysis of possible industries for my next company in 2022 and 2023. For example, recognizing AI's burgeoning impact on the accounting and educational sectors, I opted not to invest in consolidating accounting firms, and I predicted the downturn of educational services companies like Chegg.

- The companies I've led have successfully used innovation to accelerate growth that often outpaced their industry:

  » Amerex Oil Associates leveraged technology by pioneering a global IT system that enabled rapid information sharing and provided a crucial competitive advantage in the oil brokerage industry before the rise of the internet. This enabled Amerex to dominate its sector and outperform competitors, establishing an early leadership position.

» Hamilton Resources' success stemmed directly from our forward-thinking commitment to the efficient use of data. Strategic information management was central to the company's competitive differentiation and financial achievement.

» United Waste Systems capitalized on regulatory changes affecting landfill capacities and the integration of hauling and disposal by implementing sophisticated truck routing software. Our proactive adoption of this technology led to significant operational efficiencies and cost reductions. United Waste emerged as a major industry player and rapidly scaled its business.

» United Rentals identified the trend of low rental penetration in construction equipment as a major growth opportunity, strategically acquiring Wynne Systems to optimize pricing and harness asset management data. By leveraging this advanced technology, we created a distinct advantage in market penetration and operational efficiency, contributing to a swift rise to industry leadership.

» XPO strategically bet on the growing trends of "on-demand everything" and automation, hiring

Mario Harik (now CEO) to develop a fully auto-mated, digitally enabled freight transportation network. This innovation resulted in industry-leading platforms XPO Connect® and RXO Connect®, dramatically enhancing operational efficiency and customer satisfaction. XPO's spot-on trend analy-sis and the resulting technologies have led to strong industry outperformance.

Chapter 3: How to Do Lots of High-Quality M&A without Imploding

- When I negotiate a deal, I never make the seller play the waiting game. Most people find it rude. In fact, I've learned the hard way that playing games with a seller is counterproductive; just be straightforward. If you use candor with a seller instead of posturing, you're more likely to get candor in return, and that's how you get to a deal.

- I'll only do deals where the downside scenario is still good for the company, the base case is excellent, and the upside case is off the charts. And I'm not willing to accept any significant chance that an acquisition won't hit at least its base-case projections. If our analysis shows more risk than that, I'll move on.

• For me, the decision is unequivocal: If an acquisition doesn't create shareholder value by producing a high return on invested capital—if it doesn't help us thrill our customers, differentiate our offering, or fill a strategic gap—then it just makes us bigger, not better.

• M&A can dramatically accelerate growth, enhance competitive position, and drive operational efficiencies. It's the fastest and most strategic path to scaling quickly and gaining market advantages that otherwise could take years to achieve. This is especially true in fragmented industries that are ripe for consolidation.

• Generally, bigger is better in business because it provides economies of scale and a stronger market presence. However, bigger isn't universally better; some service industries thrive on local connections, agility, and personalized attention, so it's crucial to evaluate when and how scale truly benefits the business.

• Focus your acquisition strategy on industries that can produce what I call "obscene profits"—substantial returns that come from consolidating fragmented markets. Target businesses where increased scale translates into disproportionate gains, ensuring that your acquisitions are strategic, not merely incremental.

- I first heard the term "obscene profits" in a news report describing Exxon's record profits in 1979, and it sparked my interest in industries capable of massive returns. I subsequently decided to get into the oil business.

- Always stress-test your rationale behind an acquisition to ensure that it holds true even in the downside scenario. The path to outsized growth must be clear, with projections substantially higher than current performance, providing ample upside potential to justify the risks involved.

- Only hire consultants for an acquisition if the profit they're expected to add is at least 10x their fee. Focus their resources in high-impact areas—such as procurement, sales force effectiveness, and pricing strategies—to ensure a meaningful return on investment.

- The fundamental reason behind any M&A decision must always link back to enhancing customer satisfaction and driving financial performance. If acquiring a company doesn't thrill customers or create outsized financial improvement, the value creation won't be there.

- Speed is critical when you engage in competitive acquisitions, and fast execution requires thorough preparation and deep up-front research. When you're well informed going into negotiations, you can compress the due diligence time significantly, providing a crucial edge in securing valuable deals.

- At the leadership level, fast-paced M&A requires intense personal sacrifice and a relentless work ethic. Prepare yourself and your team to make large commitments of time, energy, and focus, often at the expense of comfort or personal activities, to achieve exceptional results.

- Never settle for "okay" acquisitions; these deals are more likely to hinder than help in the long run. Often, your greatest successes will stem not from the deals you close but from the mediocre ones you had the discipline to walk away from.

- Maintain control over your acquisitions by aligning your M&A strategy closely with your overall business plan and value-creation goals. Ensuring tight alignment prevents distractions. Each acquisition should contribute directly to your strategic objectives.

- Eliminate vanity from the equation. Don't pursue acquisitions to boost your image or gain temporary accolades. Each transaction should offer clear, compelling advantages that justify the complexity and capital involved, such as enhanced market position, operational synergies, or greater profitability.

- Never promise anything during negotiations that you can't deliver. Respect sellers by genuinely addressing their concerns about legacy employees, customers, and communities affected by the acquisition. Honest, respectful communication can build trust and ease tensions; convey your intentions and your sincere commitment to follow through. This often makes the difference between closing or losing a deal.

- Never assume you can force-fit cultures; always acquire companies whose cultures align with yours. A natural compatibility will foster productive change and integration; this, in turn, enables the combined culture to evolve smoothly and benefit all stakeholders.

- Be prepared for unexpected challenges when you integrate an acquisition. Prioritize completing the integration process, as delays can undermine morale, disrupt operations, and cause customer defections.

- The single most critical element in successfully integrating an acquisition is the culture part. Communicate openly with your new team members, making it clear that you value their input and will incorporate the best of their culture.

- Operational integration must emphasize speed and standardization. Quickly bring newly acquired businesses onto your existing technology platform, harmonize financial and operational systems, and standardize branding so that the integrated organization functions seamlessly as one cohesive entity.

- "Overorganize" the integration by assigning tasks to named individuals who will hold explicit accountability. Establish a regular cadence of monitoring and check-in sessions to ensure steady progress, maintain clarity on responsibilities, and quickly resolve issues before they become disruptive.

- Implement early feedback loops immediately following the acquisition to engage new employees, show respect for their insights, and surface valuable ideas. This practice not only helps identify integration issues early; it can also reveal high-caliber talent among the legacy employees.

- When speaking to employees from a company you acquire, ask them, "What's the business doing well that we'd be crazy to change?" and "What's your best idea to improve the business?" Another good question is "What's your job satisfaction on a scale of 1–10, and what would it take to make it a 10?" Succinct questions yield much better results than a lengthy survey at a busy time.

- A variation of the same questions can be used for customers: "How would you rate your satisfaction with us on a scale of 1–10, and what would it take to make it a 10?" It's important to act on the feedback you receive from customers and employees; don't just collect the data.

- At United Waste Systems, we strategically targeted tertiary markets to avoid head-on competition with major industry players. By consolidating regional landfills and local collection companies, we achieved geographic density in short order, realizing significant economies of scale and ultimately driving massive value creation.

- Dick Houston, my trusted friend and a former CIA investigator, has often vetted the management teams of acquisition targets for me. His insights notably helped us avoid acquiring a company that was later charged with serious accounting irregularities.

- At XPO, we executed three foundational acquisitions— Norbert Dentressangle, New Breed Logistics, and Con-way—over a span of just 13 months, with a combined value of more than $7 billion. The intensity of managing simultaneous integrations required extraordinary effort but ultimately delivered exceptional financial results and pervasive operational excellence.

- Once I had a memorable lunch with Hertz's CEO at the time, and he expressed frustration that United Rentals was overtaking Hertz's U.S. market position in equipment rental. It underscored how ego can impede strategic thinking and reinforced the importance of humility in making sound business decisions.

Chapter 4: How to Build an Outrageously Talented Team

- Hiring the very best people is my most critical responsibility as a CEO. I'm intentional about recruiting individuals who are exceptionally talented and who naturally collaborate constructively with their colleagues.

- A bad hire isn't merely an inconvenience; it's a costly mistake that drains resources, morale, and productivity.

I'd rather leave a position open than fill it hastily with someone who isn't the right fit. It's far easier to manage a temporary vacancy than to untangle the disruption caused by bringing in the wrong person.

- To thoroughly assess candidates, we rely on multiple methods, including rigorous interviews that can run to seven or eight rounds or more. In addition to in-depth conversations, we ask candidates to answer an extensive list of 45 questions up front, allowing us to go beyond superficial impressions in the interview. This multistep vetting process greatly improves our chances of making the right hire.

  » When I interview a candidate, I'm primarily looking for four qualities: intelligence, hunger, integrity, and collegiality. Each of these traits is indispensable, as they collectively create an environment where amazing things can happen. I won't compromise on any of these because they're the building blocks of our success.

  » Intelligence is a nonnegotiable attribute because it correlates strongly with organizational success. I'm referring to high IQ, exceptional problem-solving abilities, intellectual humility, and the capacity for dialectical thinking—considering and synthesizing different perspectives. Smart people keep the entire organization learning and moving forward. Spencer Stuart's study on IQ versus EQ confirmed that high IQ correlates most strongly with organizational success, which aligns with my prioritizing intelligence when hiring. While emotional intelligence has value, raw intellectual horsepower is indispensable for driving business results at scale.

» Hunger refers to a person's drive and tenacity—the willingness to put in the extra effort, work hard (even nights and weekends), and remain resilient in challenging situations. I look for people who are motivated not just by a desire to achieve but also by the potential to earn substantial financial rewards. Lean, slightly understaffed teams composed of driven individuals maintain better focus and consistently deliver results.

» Integrity is a must-have quality because trust is fundamental to a winning team. People with integrity follow through on their commitments and never need to boast about being honest; their actions speak for them. Conversely, hiring someone who lacks integrity isn't just a risk; it's an existential threat to the business and its reputational value.

» Collegiality is crucial for creating a productive and supportive workplace. People who are kind and cooperative help a business thrive through collaboration, while those who engage in cutthroat tactics rarely find a lasting place on our team. I aim for an environment where people genuinely enjoy each other's company.

- We actively manage our talent using an A, B, C player evaluation system. The A players are indispensable assets who make significant contributions, while B players deliver acceptable performance and have the potential to improve. C players are consistently underperforming, are misaligned with the company's values, or both; they must be transitioned out.

- One way I evaluate talent is to conduct a thought experiment where I imagine the employee suddenly walking into my office to resign. I gauge my immediate emotional reaction: Relief indicates they're a C player I'd replace anyway, mild disappointment but acceptance indicates a B player, and outright panic signals an A player whose departure would be a major loss.

- I've learned from mentors such as Wayland Hicks the importance of being firm yet compassionate when exiting C players. A generous exit package can maintain the employee's dignity. At the same time, it's important to be decisive because one person's chronic underperformance can bring down morale and productivity. This balanced approach maintains trust with the broader team.

- My companies "overpay" employees, particularly direct reports, as a conscious strategy to ensure we attract and retain the best talent. By aligning compensation with clearly defined strategic goals and tangible value creation, employees feel invested in the company's success. Well-designed incentive structures motivate people to exceed expectations.

- Our incentive plans encourage employees to push their limits, motivating them to go as far and as fast as they can. As a general practice, we avoid placing caps on compensation because we want to fully reward exceptional performance. High-performing people can see the correlation between their efforts and the tangible rewards they receive.

- Equity incentives that are extended throughout the organizational chart create a sense of shared ownership in a company's success. When employees hold equity, they understand their personal stake in our strategic outcomes. This enhances retention and loyalty. It's an intentional way to build a cohesive, committed team.

- My own interviewing process underscores my commitment to interpersonal connections and a cultural fit. I interview every new employee who will be based at our headquarters to ensure they align with our core values and are a good fit with the existing team. These interviews have been essential in shaping the culture of our corporate team.

- My successor CEOs at XPO, GXO, and RXO come from different backgrounds, but they share the four critical qualities I noted: intelligence, hunger, integrity, and collegiality. The cultures we built together remain strong. Their outstanding leadership highlights the universal importance of these key traits.

- With Amerex, we sought highly driven individuals who were "close to broke" and therefore very motivated to succeed. Their hunger, driven by financial necessity, significantly contributed to the company's rapid growth and success, as well as their own. Scrappy determination has consistently been a hallmark of our most successful teams.

- Entrepreneur Dick Colburn, the founder of U.S. Rentals, emphasized the critical role of compensation and profit sharing in achieving business success. U.S. Rentals was publicly traded under his leadership when United Rentals acquired the company. Colburn's philosophy greatly influenced my perspective on incentivizing employees generously to align their interests with strategy.

- At XPO, we successfully attracted talent from top-tier companies like Alphabet, Amazon, and Goldman Sachs by offering highly competitive compensation packages and compelling incentive structures. This recruiting strategy ensured we built a team with world-class capabilities, and it has been a major factor in driving superior company performance.

Chapter 5: How to Run Electric Meetings

- My education at Bennington College in the 1970s was a formative experience that cemented my preference for intellectually challenging discussions instead of passive lectures. This, in turn, shaped my philosophy on conducting engaging business meetings.

- I avoid falling prey to "big company-itis," which leads to dull, bureaucratic meetings that stifle creativity and productivity. Instead, I embrace unpredictability and foster environments where dynamic discussions thrive, bringing real value to each interaction.

- Electric meetings have three essential elements: the right people in the room, a crowdsourced agenda, and an atmosphere where everyone feels secure enough to disagree respectfully. These elements keep meetings engaging and productive.

- I intentionally keep most meetings small—around 15 to 20 attendees—to encourage authentic discussions and minimize unnecessary posturing. It's a large enough group to draw out a diversity of perspectives while ensuring that everyone participates in a meaningful way.

- I typically invite a diverse mix of attendees to meetings—senior executives, subject-matter experts, and promising newcomers—to ensure that everyone has a sense of what's happening across the company, not just within their own area. This enriches discussions, broadens perspectives, and leads to more productive outcomes.

- I insist on participation from all attendees, emphasizing that passive listening equates to taking without giving. Everyone leaves the meeting with new insights.

- I select my meeting moderators thoughtfully, sometimes choosing "surprise moderators" from different parts of the business to keep the discussions fresh. The goal is to guide the conversation productively, allowing new perspectives to surface and keeping the vibe energized and impartial.

- Another technique I use is to crowdsource the meeting's agenda by circulating slide decks in advance and soliciting participants' critical takeaways and questions. Ranking these inputs helps shape an agenda focused on meaningful discussion points.

- Meetings should have only a few rules: devices off, one person speaking at a time, undivided attention, and respectful disagreement. These simple guidelines ensure that meetings remain efficient and productive.

- Enforce the rules by demonstrating there are firm consequences for disruptions. For example, I once temporarily banned XPO's chief customer officer from our regular operating reviews because of his side conversations; it drove home the importance of respecting meeting rules.

- Meeting attendees should avoid sugarcoating or withholding unpleasant news. Honest and unfiltered communication, even when it's about negative developments, gives senior leadership clarity and helps build confidence across the organization.

- I foster succession planning through operating reviews by giving executives insights into various parts of the company beyond their sphere and spotlighting emerging talent. Regular exposure to different departments helps identify potential future leaders and prepares them for larger roles.

- Monthly and quarterly operating reviews are the backbone of organizational alignment. They serve as essential platforms for communication, operational oversight, and value creation.

- I conduct board meetings with the same commitment to open communication as internal meetings. This reinforces mutual trust and productive oversight.

- My team applies crowdsourcing principles to town halls with our wider organization, allowing the audience to set agendas through spontaneous Q&A sessions. This approach greatly increases engagement, making the time more rewarding for participants.

- I favor an open-ended, spontaneous style for communication whenever possible such as my "ask me anything" approach to external events like fireside chats. This is another way to communicate my commitment to candid dialogue.

- Embracing respectful disagreement is a healthy part of the communication process. I actively encourage conflicting opinions during meetings. Evidence-based discussions allow the group to leverage its collective expertise, and a range of perspectives elevates the debate. This leads to breakthrough insights and more informed decisions.

- The most effective way to challenge someone's idea is to pair feedback with supportive acknowledgment. This approach shows empathy, reduces defensiveness, and creates a positive environment for productive discussions.

- As CEO, I sometimes exert executive privilege to make unilateral decisions that differ from the group's consensus, but only after carefully listening to others' opinions and explaining my rationale.

- End each meeting on a positive note by highlighting successes and recognizing contributions. Ask attendees whose star rose highest during the discussion; it motivates everyone to perform their best.

Chapter 6: How to Kill the Competition Instead of Killing Each Other

- A customer relationship is like any other relationship: to improve it, you first have to let the other party know you value it. One way to do this is through a combination of respectful listening and nonjudgmental concentration. Mirror back to the customer what they've told you about the relationship: what they like and what could be improved. Then, take concrete steps to better the relationship based on the customer's feedback.

- A unified team culture is imperative to a company's success because it aligns employees with ambitious goals. When someone feels part of something larger and understands their role within it, their performance elevates.

- People naturally want to be associated with exciting endeavors. Providing clarity to employees about their contributions helps them realize that each person has importance, and this fosters a deeper commitment to the vision.

- Collaboration remains the most powerful mechanism for driving a company's strategic goals forward. By emphasizing seamless teamwork across departments, organizations can unlock potential that far exceeds what individuals can achieve alone.

- We can learn valuable lessons from superorganisms like ant colonies and bacterial networks, which showcase advanced systems of communication, clear divisions of labor, and precise coordination in decision-making. These natural examples demonstrate how, collectively, effective communication can lead to superior outcomes.

- Regular communication through multiple internal channels such as emails, social media, town halls, and site visits strengthens company-wide trust. Consistent "overcommunication" inspires employees, keeps everyone informed, and fosters a robust internal community.

- Giving board members unrestricted access to the organization, including company executives and internal data, strengthens fiduciary oversight and builds mutual trust. This approach also ensures accountability and aligns management's actions with shareholders' interests.

- Sincere listening—being actively and deeply attentive to others—and acting on insights are both essential skills for continuous improvement. Listening builds strong connections and channels frontline insights to leadership, which in turn benefit strategic decision-making and organizational performance.

- Implementing comprehensive company-wide feedback loops, like regular employee surveys, ensures unfiltered input. Feedback loops give employees a meaningful voice, help surface critical issues, and flag areas for immediate action.

- By sharing survey findings openly with all employees, even when the comments are critical, management communicates that employee feedback is genuinely valued. This can accelerate organizational growth. Critiques received from disgruntled employees often point to underlying organizational issues. By carefully considering the feedback, you can identify areas of concern that merit attention.

- When a company expands its communications beyond internal audiences to include external groups—customers, investors, industry media, the public—it helps maintain strategic alignment, manage expectations, and foster productive relationships. This enhances the company's credibility.

- Robust customer feedback loops allow the company to proactively manage customer expectations, gather critical usage data, and provide meaningful consultations. Customer relationships are rooted in mutual benefit, and feedback loops can create more loyal partnerships.

- During crises, proactive investor communication is crucial for maintaining investor trust and managing expectations. Open dialogue can forestall erosion of investor confidence and help stabilize company performance.

- There's a perceived conflict between delivering high quality and delivering at high speed, yet world-class organizations consistently accomplish both. Successful companies refuse to accept this false trade-off, insisting instead on simultaneous excellence.

- My understanding of communication and collaboration was significantly influenced by the book *The Superorganism* by Bert Holldobler and E. O. Wilson. It details how social insects achieve high-level team effectiveness through sophisticated communication. It's analogous to the importance of coordination and division of labor in companies.

- Jazz musician Bill Dixon exemplified how improvisational experimentation can draw out the best in each member of a team. His approach underscored the value of creating spaces where others feel comfortable taking risks and expressing innovative ideas freely.

- Marina Abramović's performance art piece *The Artist Is Present* demonstrated the transformative power of providing undivided, nonjudgmental attention to others. This concept, applied within a business, emphasizes the profound impact of truly listening and connecting deeply with colleagues.

- GXO Logistics, an XPO spin-off, applied best practices from its top-performing warehouses to its entire network to enhance overall organizational performance. By leveraging these frontline insights, the GXO team ensured pervasive operational excellence.

- In 2019, XPO's largest customer abruptly withdrew $600 million in annual business. We navigated this crisis with radical acceptance and clear communication to all stakeholders. This approach ultimately led to revenue recovery and an increase in our stock value, demonstrating the strength of proactive communication in times of adversity.

- If you're going to pursue making a few billion dollars, you'll want to give some thought to your own best path to creating a collaborative culture with open communication.

Conclusion

- Life's greatest rewards are achievable when you fully commit yourself to your passions, boldly embrace change, and actively accept responsibility for creating your own purpose. Hard work is the cornerstone of a deeply satisfying and purposeful life.

- My personal priorities are my family, robust and diverse experiences that enhance my understanding of life, and the meaningful work I pursue. While each is vitally important to me, I hold family and life experience slightly above work, as they form the foundation upon which all my business endeavors are built.

- In business, true success arises from the ability to anticipate significant trends, build highly talented teams, pursue value-enhancing mergers and acquisitions, drive robust growth, and, importantly, reorient thinking to enable creative problem-solving. This comprehensive approach has allowed me to repeatedly deliver outstanding results.

- My fundamental drive comes from the fulfillment I experience in turning ambitious ideas into tangible realities. This satisfaction extends beyond financial rewards to the meaningful impacts my ventures have on countless people well outside the borders of my companies.

- As fiduciaries, I believe that the essential responsibility of business leaders is to create shareholder value by making strategic decisions that drive long-term growth. We must ensure healthy workplaces for employees, provide exceptional service to customers, operate within the law, and face inevitable challenges with practical optimism.

» At United Waste Systems, we created substantial shareholder value while simultaneously making America a cleaner, healthier place. Our growth provided numerous small businesses with financially beneficial exit opportunities, enabling them to enjoy well-earned rewards from their entrepreneurial efforts.

» At United Rentals, our investments in innovations transformed logistics, elevated worker safety standards, and improved equipment utilization. These improvements not only created superior value for our shareholders but also reduced the environmental footprint of the industries we served.

» XPO and its spin-offs have revolutionized supply chain management through advanced technology developments, directly benefiting manufacturers, retailers, and consumers alike. The resulting operational efficiencies have boosted profits and productivity while also benefiting the environment.

- When I received a message from a hedge fund owner thanking me for the $500 million of incremental value generated by XPO stock in his fund, it underscored for me that our success enriches the lives of ordinary people. In this case, the wealth primarily supported members of pension plans and university endowments—a far-reaching impact of our efforts.

- The core of the entrepreneurial spirit is composed of an unwavering work ethic, a relentless focus on customer satisfaction, an ability to outsmart competitors, and the generation of wealth that benefits people, families, and communities. It's a mindset that thrives on innovation, with an enthusiasm for seizing opportunities.

- I want to mention Steve, my HVAC technician, because he perfectly embodies the entrepreneurial spirit with his commitment, admirable work ethic, and customer-centric approach. His pride in craftsmanship and his comfort with openly pursuing profit exemplify the virtues of a true entrepreneur.

- I wrote this book for people who want to work their tails off, outsmart the competition, put their customers on a pedestal, and make a lot of money for their families. These goals require creativity and an enthusiasm for change—two more attributes at the heart of entrepreneurship. You can foster this spirit in any organization, whether you're the owner of a family business or the CEO of a multibillion-dollar company looking to create its next billion.

- My time at the Rhode Island Governor's School for the Gifted in Art and Music profoundly shaped my approach to life and business. The summer program fostered my creativity and willingness to take risks, sharpened my time-management skills, and taught me how to maintain motivation. Most importantly, I learned the value of fully committing myself—going all in to achieve extraordinary goals.

- I came away from that experience knowing that it's in our own hands to make life meaningful or just pass the time until we die. We're not at the mercy of others when it comes to experiencing how enriching life can be. That's up to each of us, and it depends on how much we're willing to work at it.

- I'm inspired daily by people I see charging toward their passion, in some cases despite enormous challenges. I have faith they'll persevere because I believe that people who push for extraordinary outcomes are inherently winners, embodying the traits I've described in this book.

Timeline of Unnatural Selection

COULD THE DARWINIAN MODEL of evolution be giving way to an AI-based paradigm? The day may come when the evolution of our species no longer depends solely on mutations of DNA but instead is driven by a merging of natural selection and "unnatural selection"—a process driven by the introduction of new tools and technologies. Here's a list of what I consider to be the most consequential tools and technologies developed by humans over the course of 2.6 million years, including the breathtaking acceleration of innovation in the last 75 years.

How to Make a Few *More* Billion Dollars

2.6 million years ago	Oldowan stone tools by *Homo habilis*, early human ancestors
1.7 million years ago	Acheulean hand axes by protohuman *Homo erectus*
1.5 million years ago	Specialized bone tools
1 million years ago	Controlled use of fire by *Homo erectus*
65,000 BC	Bow and arrow
10,000 BC	Agricultural tools
4,000 BC	Plow
3,500 BC	Bronze tools and weapons (start of Bronze Age)
3,500 BC	Wheel and axle
3,200 BC	Writing systems (cuneiform and hieroglyphics)
3,000 BC	Sail-powered navigation
1,200 BC	Iron tools (start of Iron Age)
1,000 BC	Concrete
250 BC	Compound pulley (Archimedes)

250 BC	Watermills and aqueducts
105 AD	Papermaking
800 AD	Windmills
9th century AD	Gunpowder
11th century AD	Compass
1260	Mechanical clock
1290	Eyeglasses
1440	Printing press (Gutenberg)
1590	Microscope
1609	Astronomical telescope (Galileo)
1642	Mechanical calculator (Pascal)
1656	Pendulum clock
1712	Steam engine
1755	Textile roller-spinning machine
1796	Smallpox vaccine
1800	Electric battery

1804	Steam-powered locomotive train
1816	Stethoscope
1826	Photographic camera
1831	Electrical generator
1834	Vapor-compression refrigeration system
1837	Telegraph (Morse)
1860	Internal combustion engine
1867	Dynamite (Nobel)
1868	Typewriter
1876	Telephone (Bell)
1879	Long-lasting light bulb and electrical system (Edison)
1886	Automobile
1895	X-ray imaging
1896	Wireless radiotelegraphy (Marconi)
1898	Electric hearing aid
1902	Modern air conditioning

1903	Powered aircraft (Wright brothers)
1907	Fully synthetic plastic
1913	Assembly line (Ford)
1924	Electroencephalogram or EEG
1928	Discovery of penicillin (Fleming)
1935	Radar
1939	Television
1943	Nuclear reactor
1945	General-purpose electronic computer (ENIAC)
1945	Atomic bomb
1945	Microwave oven
1947	Transistor
1948	Stored-program computer
1949	Commercial jet airliner
1950	Military-level drones
1954	Industrial robot

How to Make a Few *More* Billion Dollars

1957   Artificial satellite (Sputnik)

1959   Silicon chip

1958   Cardiac pacemaker

1960s Fiber optics

1960   Laser

1968   Virtual reality system with head-mounted display

1969   Internet prototype (ARPANET)

1969   Computer-controlled robotic arm

1971   Email

1971   Microprocessor (Intel)

1971   Pocket calculator (Texas Instruments)

1973   Global Positioning System

1973   Mobile telephone (Motorola)

1977   Magnetic resonance imaging

1978   In vitro fertilization

1981   Personal computer (IBM)

1981   Nanotechnology

1983   Internet

1986   3D printing

1986   Autonomous vehicle

1990   Internet search engine (Archie)

1990   Commercial voice recognition system (Dragon Dictate)

1990   Human gene therapy

1991   World Wide Web and websites

1992   Videoconferencing

1995   Windows 95

1996   Cloned mammal (Dolly the sheep)

1998   Google search engine

1998   Facial recognition

2003   Human Genome Project completed

2006   Public cloud service (Amazon Web Services)

2007   iPhone (Apple)

2008	Collaborative warehouse robots (cobots)
2008	Carbon nanotubes for targeted chemotherapy
2009	Blockchain and Bitcoin networks
2011	Breakthrough in AI (IBM's Watson)
2012	Gene editing tool (CRISPR-Cas9)
2015	Reusable rocket (SpaceX)
2016	DeepMind AlphaGo AI defeats human Go champion
2017	CAR-T immunotherapy engineered for cancer cells
2019	Quantum computing supremacy over supercomputers (Google's Sycamore)
2020	mRNA vaccines for COVID-19
2021	James Webb Space Telescope
2021	AI mapping of protein structures (Google's AlphaFold)
2023	GPT-4 large language model AI (OpenAI)

Humanity's 13.8-Billion-Year Profit and Loss Statement

IN BUSINESS, ONE OF the most important financial documents is the profit and loss (P&L) statement, which typically spans the past three years. It provides a clear view of a company's financial evolution, including the key factors that shaped its current position. In a similar spirit, what follows is the "P&L of human existence," an account tracing the trajectory of human evolution from a singularity 13.8 billion years ago, at the moment of the Big Bang, to the present day.

13.8 billion years ago	Singularity
The first trillionth of a second after the Big Bang	Elementary particles
13.79 billion years ago	Atoms
13.7 billion years ago	Stars
13 billion years ago	Heavy elements
4.5 billion years ago	Formation of Earth
3.56 billion years ago	Prokaryotes
2 billion years ago	Eukaryotes
655 million years ago	Sponges and comb jellies
600 million years ago	Flatworms
510 million years ago	Fish
365 million years ago	Amphibians

Humanity's 13.8-Billion-Year Profit and Loss Statement

300 million years ago	Synapsid reptiles
250 million years ago	Cynodonts
65 million years ago	Small mammals
57 to 55 million years ago	Plesiadapiformes
57 million years ago	Primates
25 million years ago	Great apes
7 million years ago	Hominids
2.2 million years ago	*Homo habilis*
2 million years ago	*Homo erectus*
300,000 years ago	*Homo sapiens*
???	"Techno sapiens"

Thought Experiments

GEDANKENEXPERIMENTS, or thought experiments, are mental simulations to expand your mind. They can spark creativity, lead to aha moments, and provide context for tackling big challenges. That context can sharpen your perspective and help you achieve life-changing business and personal goals. Here are a few examples of thought experiments to inspire your own:

- Imagine the beginning of time—an incomprehensibly dense singularity erupting in a burst of energy and expansion. Every elementary particle in existence comes into being at this moment, forming the raw material for everything that will ever be. Visualize hydrogen atoms forming first, then clumping into stars under the force of gravity. Watch as these stars live out their cycles, fusing heavy elements in their cores and exploding in supernovae that scatter matter across space. Picture these particles shooting through the universe—colliding, joining, and separating for billions of years. Eventually, some of them coalesce to form planets, oceans, and life. Now see those same particles that once spun in galactic clouds becoming your bones, your fingernails, the oxygen in your lungs. Feel your connection to all things—humans, chimpanzees, bananas, flowers, stars. You are not merely part of the universe; you are its direct continuation. Every cell, every atom in your body, has traveled across time and space to arrive at this moment, carrying the story of creation within it.

- Picture a star exploding 5 billion years ago, spewing gaseous clouds and particulate matter into the vastness of the universe at the end of its life. Over a few hundred million years, some of that stardust comes together under the pressure of gravity and forms our Sun and

Solar System. Visualize everything in our Solar System, including Earth, forming from that reconfigured stardust. Allow your frame of consciousness to expand out from your one-foot-diameter head to the farthest reaches of the Solar System—all 22 trillion miles of it. Imagine yourself not as the trillions of cells in your body or the trillions of synaptic connections in your brain but as the entire Solar System. We are all made of elements that originated from the same stars that blew up billions of years ago. Picture everything you've ever seen or touched as originating from that same stardust.

- The expansion of the universe is accelerating faster and faster over time, so if you were born far into the future, you would see a lot less of the universe than you can see now. The universe might be expanding so fast that in the distant future, nothing will be visible beyond our Milky Way and the Andromeda Galaxy. Everything else may be too far away to observe. Picture yourself hundreds of billions of years in the future, so far into the future that the majority of our present universe has drifted too far away for light to reach you, traveling at a finite speed. You can get information about our observable universe, but there's now a huge amount of matter in what's become the unobservable universe. See what you'll experience as you let your mind wander between these two worlds, one observable and the other not.

- Visualize not just one universe but an infinite number of universes—the multiverse. You're in all places at one time, like a traveler on a long journey who has simultaneously reached all possible destinations. You're omniscient and omnipotent in a multiverse that exists in an infinite number of dimensions.

- Allow your awareness to be in your whole body from head to toe; then begin to drift inward. Pass through your skin into a world of fibers, capillaries, and pulsing cells. Enter one cell, passing through the plasma membrane, and see the intricate machinery that keeps it alive: endoplasmic reticula, ribosomes, mitochondria. Enter the cell nucleus, and observe the spirals of DNA around you. Dive deeper into a single atom within that DNA, crossing the vast emptiness between electrons and the nucleus until you reach the protons and neutrons. Let yourself go farther still, into the quarks and gluons—the smallest known building blocks—where all matter is held together in a constant dance of energy. Here, at this scale, feel the constant subtle fluctuations that underlie your existence. From the smallest quantum entities—whether particles or waves—to your entire body, everything is part of the same continuous quantum fabric, holding you in this moment.

- Try to picture your body in all its microscopic complexity. It's composed of more than 30 trillion human cells and even more bacterial cells. All these cells are alive and smarter than you might think—and they're constantly in the process of being born, living, and dying. Visualize your stomach cells being replaced every week. See brand-new skin cells appearing monthly. Picture red blood cells carrying oxygen to every part of your body being renewed every four months. Envision your liver cells undergoing a complete renewal every nine months. Get closely in tune with the everchanging rhythms of your body's life.

- Imagine yourself as a single-celled prokaryotic bacterium in Earth's primordial oceans about 4 billion years ago. You evolve into more complex eukaryotic cells, merging respiration and photosynthesis. You develop into a sponge, the first multicellular organism, then into a flatworm with bilateral symmetry—a precursor to organ systems. Over time, your lineage becomes fish with skulls, brains, and limbs, then amphibians venturing onto land. Eventually, you're a synapsid reptile, then a cynodont mammal. You gain warm-blooded traits and a larger brain. You scurry through trees as a plesiadapiform, then evolve into a primate with color vision and dexterous hands. As a great ape, you develop a more complex brain. You walk upright as a hominid, losing your tail and facial fur. As a protohuman, you make tools, hunt, cook, and communicate through gestures and sound. Finally, as *Homo sapiens*, you acquire language, art, and culture. Experience yourself as the culmination of this multibillion-year journey—from a prokaryotic bacterium to a conscious human being.

- Picture the entire universe running backward. Galaxies drift closer together, stars collapse into swirling gas clouds, planets disassemble into dust, and life recedes into simpler forms. Trees shrink into seeds, seeds dissolve into soil, and the soil separates into minerals. Humans lose their languages, tools, and stories, becoming hunter-gatherers, then primates, then early mammals scurrying through ferns. Keep rewinding until oceans evaporate into the air, continents merge, the Earth itself crumbles into particles, and stars retreat into the dark void. Finally, watch as all space, matter, and time compress into a single, infinitesimally dense point—a singularity. In that stillness, feel the universe inhale, holding its breath before the birth of another beginning.

- Conceive of a future in which the universe has grown incomprehensibly old. The stars have dimmed, black holes have released their last whispers of energy, and the cosmos is a peaceful sea of darkness. Yet in this deep future, you remain a conscious being, holding within you the memory of everything that ever was. You drift through the stillness with the warm memory of sextillions of glowing suns. With a single thought, you plant the seed of another universe and blissfully watch as light blooms again, synthesizing your memories into a fresh infinity. Imagine a warm, gentle light pulsating in your heart, radiating pure love. With each heartbeat, feel the light grow warmer, filling you with deep gratitude for the people and moments that bring you joy. Let that feeling of gratitude gently spread throughout your entire body, creating a sense of peace and happiness in every cell.

Sources of Equity Capital

ENTREPRENEURS OFTEN MAKE THE mistake of abandoning a strong business plan because they get stuck on the question of how to raise the necessary capital. This is unfortunate. There are countless institutions and individuals actively seeking to invest substantial money where it can generate attractive returns. In this appendix alone, you'll find an estimated $30 *trillion* in capital looking for a home—and that's just from sources I happen to be familiar with.

Disclaimer: I've made my best effort to provide accurate figures as of publication, but the exact numbers for these funds are difficult to pin down. Many funds do not disclose their assets under management (AUM). The amounts below reflect rough estimates of equity AUM only—the amount each organization dedicates specifically to equity investments. Allocations to bonds, credit, and other debt instruments are excluded, as is the share of AUM that I believe is passively invested (e.g., index funds, ETFs). Furthermore, these figures fluctuate daily with market movements and can change significantly from year to year. However, the main point remains: There's a vast amount of capital in the world, and a need for funding should never be the reason to abandon a solid business idea. The world is constrained by a lack of great ideas, not by a lack of capital.

Family Offices

Walton Enterprises	$225 billion
Bessemer Trust Company (Phipps family and others)	$200 billion
Bezos Expeditions	$108 billion
Al Saud Company	$100 billion
Bayshore Global Management (Sergey Brin)	$100 billion
Excession (Elon Musk)	$100 billion
Mousse Partners (Alain and Gérard Wertheimer)	$90 billion
Ballmer Group (Steve Ballmer)	$85 billion

Family Offices continued

ICONIQ Capital (Mark Zuckerberg and others)	$80 billion
Dubai Holding (Sheikh Mohammed bin Rashid Al Maktoum)	$72 billion
Cascade (Bill Gates)	$70 billion
Waycrosse (Cargill-MacMillan family)	$65 billion
Fedesa (Ferrero family)	$55 billion
Pontegadea Inversiones (Amancio Ortega)	$54 billion
AC Limited (Al Nahyan family)	$50 billion
Financière Agache (Bernard Arnault)	$40 billion
Athos (Andreas and Thomas Strüngmann)	$31 billion
DFO (Michael Dell)	$31 billion
Delfin (Leonardo Del Vecchio)	$30 billion
Emerson Collective (Laurene Powell Jobs)	$28 billion
Soros Fund Management	$28 billion
Rockefeller Global Family Office	$27 billion
Tata Capital	$27 billion
26North (Josh and Marjorie Harris)	$25 billion
LTS Investments (Jorge Paulo Lemann, Marcel Telles, and Carlos Sicupira)	$25 billion
Willett Advisors (Michael Bloomberg)	$25 billion
Stonehage Fleming (Fleming family)	$23 billion
Hartono (Robert Budi and Michael Hartono)	$21 billion
Access Industries (Len Blavatnik)	$20 billion
Krefeld Invest (Hermès family)	$20 billion

How to Make a Few *More* Billion Dollars

Family Offices continued

Koch Investment Companies	$20 billion
Grupo Carso (Carlos Slim)	$20 billion
Crosby Advisors (Johnson family)	$17 billion
J. Safra Group	$17 billion
Pritzker Private Capital	$15 billion
A. P. Moller Holding (Møller family)	$14 billion
Meritage (Nat Simons)	$12 billion
Cercano (Paul Allen's estate and others)	$10 billion
KIRKBI (Kristiansen family)	$10 billion
Madrone Capital Partners (Walton family)	$10 billion
Alta Advisers (Rausing family)	$10 billion
Exor (Agnelli family)	$10 billion
RCap (Michael Rubin)	$10 billion
The Olayan Group (Hutham and Lubna Olayan)	$10 billion
Ziff Brothers (Dirk, Robert, and Daniel Ziff)	$10 billion
KrisDan Management (Reinhold Schmieding)	$7 billion
Builders Vision (Lucas Walton)	$5 billion
JAWS Estates Capital (Barry Sternlicht)	$5 billion
EOTHEN (Stavros Niarchos)	$5 billion

Sovereign Wealth Funds

Abu Dhabi Investment Authority (UAE)	$500 billion
GIC (Singapore)	$500 billion

Sovereign Wealth Funds continued

Public Investment Fund (Saudi Arabia)	$442 billion
Temasek (Singapore)	$339 billion
Mubadala (UAE)	$330 billion
Kuwait Investment Authority	$300 billion
Qatar Investment Authority	$225 billion
Investment Corporation of Dubai	$200 billion
Korea Investment Corporation	$189 billion
ADQ (UAE)	$125 billion
Oman Investment Authority	$26 billion
Mumtalakat (Bahrain)	$9 billion

Pension Funds

Canada Pension Plan Investment Board (CPPIB)	$250 billion
Public Sector Pension Investment Board (PSP)	$220 billion
California Public Employees' Retirement System (CalPERS)	$148 billion
AustralianSuper	$101 billion
La Caisse (formerly Caisse de dépôt et placement du Québec)	$97 billion
New York State Common Retirement Fund	$89 billion
California State Teachers' Retirement System (CalSTRS)	$83 billion
Ontario Teachers' Pension Plan	$65 billion
Washington State Department of Retirement Systems	$62 billion

How to Make a Few *More* Billion Dollars

British Columbia Investment Management Corporation (BCI)	$60 billion
State of Wisconsin Investment Board (SWIB)	$53 billion
Florida State Board of Administration	$53 billion
Teacher Retirement System of Texas	$51 billion
New York State Teachers' Retirement System (NYSTRS)	$48 billion
Healthcare of Ontario Pension Plan (HOOPP)	$47 billion
Ontario Municipal Employees Retirement System (OMERS)	$40 billion
Alberta Investment Management Corporation (AIMCo)	$40 billion
Minnesota State Board of Investment	$40 billion
Virginia Retirement System	$39 billion
Nevada Public Employees' Retirement System (NVPERS)	$32 billion
Ohio Public Employees Retirement System (OPERS)	$30 billion
The Retirement Systems of Alabama	$28 billion
State Teachers Retirement System of Ohio	$27 billion
Tennessee Consolidated Retirement System (TCRS)	$26 billion
Michigan Department of Treasury Bureau of Investments	$25 billion
North Carolina Retirement Systems (NCRS)	$25 billion
New Zealand Superannuation Fund	$24 billion
Oregon Public Employees Retirement System	$24 billion
Pennsylvania State Employees' Retirement System	$20 billion

Pension Funds continued

UniSuper (Australia)	$20 billion
South Carolina Retirement System (SCRS)	$18 billion
Texas Municipal Retirement System (TMRS)	$15 billion
Investment Management Corporation of Ontario (IMCO)	$14 billion
Arizona Public Safety Personnel Retirement System	$9 billion
Municipal Employees' Retirement System of Michigan	$8 billion
State Universities Retirement System of Illinois	$8 billion
Maryland State Retirement and Pension System (MSRA)	$6 billion

Endowments

Harvard University	$30 billion
Yale University	$25 billion
Stanford University	$22 billion
Princeton University	$20 billion
University of Texas System	$19 billion
University of California System	$18 billion
University of Notre Dame	$17 billion
MIT	$15 billion
Northwestern University	$14 billion
Columbia University	$14 billion
Duke University	$13 billion

How to Make a Few *More* Billion Dollars

Endowments continued

Texas A&M University	$12 billion
Washington University in St. Louis	$12 billion
Johns Hopkins University	$11 billion
Emory University	$10 billion
Cornell University	$10 billion
University of Chicago	$10 billion
University of Michigan	$9 billion
University of Pennsylvania	$7 billion
Dartmouth College	$5 billion

Long-Only Funds

Fidelity Management & Research	$4 trillion
BlackRock	$2.9 trillion
Wellington	$1.3 trillion
T. Rowe Price Associates	$1.2 trillion
Capital World	$1 trillion
Capital International	$700 billion
Legal & General Investment Management	$670 billion
Franklin Templeton	$656 billion
Columbia Threadneedle	$650 billion
Goldman Sachs Asset Management	$650 billion
Northern Trust Asset Management	$615 billion
Capital Research	$600 billion

Long-Only Funds continued

Morgan Stanley Investment Management	$535 billion
Amundi Asset Management	$500 billion
MFS Investment Management	$345 billion
AllianceBernstein	$343 billion
Nomura Asset Management	$329 billion
Berkshire Hathaway	$318 billion
Nuveen	$317 billion
Invesco	$287 billion
Janus Henderson	$243 billion
Macquarie Investment Management	$243 billion
Fisher Investments	$237 billion
Dodge & Cox	$235 billion
BNY Investments	$215 billion
HSBC Asset Management	$214 billion
American Century	$203 billion
Brookfield Asset Management	$200 billion
Manulife Investment Management	$200 billion
Principal Global Investors	$196 billion
ClearBridge Investments	$195 billion
UBS Asset Management	$193 billion
SEB Asset Management	$190 billion
RBC Global Asset Management	$187 billion
Schroders Investments	$179 billion
Daiwa Asset Management	$175 billion

How to Make a Few *More* Billion Dollars

T. Rowe Price Investment Management	$175 billion
US Bancorp Asset Management	$175 billion
Jennison Associates	$175 billion
TD Asset Management (TDAM)	$168 billion
Swedbank Robur Fonder	$167 billion
DWS Asset Management	$166 billion
Nordea Asset Management	$146 billion
BNP Paribas	$145 billion
Neuberger Berman	$142 billion
Putnam Investment Management	$142 billion
Fidelity International	$137 billion
Union Investment	$136 billion
Aegon USA	$132 billion
Allianz	$131 billion
Pictet Asset Management	$130 billion
PRIMECAP Management Company	$125 billion
Allspring Global Investments	$125 billion
Artisan Partners	$122 billion
WCM Investment Management	$116 billion
Boston Partners	$115 billion
APG Asset Management	$105 billion
Deka Investments	$104 billion
First Eagle Investment Management	$100 billion

Sources of Equity Capital

Long-Only Funds continued

Voya Investment Management	$100 billion
Loomis Sayles	$90 billion
Federated Hermes	$89 billion
Royal London Asset Management	$89 billion
Robeco Institutional	$88 billion
Lazard Asset Management	$82 billion
Capital International	$80 billion
Citi Investment Management	$80 billion
Harris Associates	$79 billion
Mitsubishi UFJ	$77 billion
Mackenzie Investments Corporation	$77 billion
Fidelity Investments Canada	$76 billion
Brown Advisory	$75 billion
Anima Holding	$70 billion
Grantham, Mayo, Van Otterloo & Co.	$63 billion
M&G Investments	$61 billion
AXA	$60 billion
Ensign Peak Advisors	$58 billion
City National Rochdale	$56 billion
CI Global Asset Management	$53 billion
Aristotle Capital Management	$49 billion
Ninety One Asset Management	$48 billion
Mirae Asset Global Investments	$47 billion

How to Make a Few *More* Billion Dollars

PineStone Asset Management	$45 billion
Causeway Capital Management	$42 billion
William Blair Investment Management	$40 billion
AMF Fonder AB	$40 billion
Thornburg Investment Management	$40 billion
Orbis Investment Management	$40 billion
Aberdeen Investments	$38 billion
Fayez Sarofim	$38 billion
Baron Capital	$37 billion
VanEck Associates	$35 billion
First Manhattan	$34 billion
Sands Capital	$34 billion
Julius Baer	$32 billion
Artemis Investment Management	$32 billion
MassMutual Life Insurance	$30 billion
Lord, Abbett & Co	$30 billion
Barrow Hanley	$30 billion
BBVA Asset Management	$28 billion
Calamos Investments	$28 billion
Vontobel Asset Management	$28 billion
BMO Global Asset Management	$25 billion
Winslow Capital Management	$25 billion
AGF Investments	$25 billion

Sources of Equity Capital

Long-Only Funds continued

Pacific Investment Management Company (PIMCO)	$24 billion
J O Hambro	$22 billion
Luther King Capital Management	$21 billion
Wasatch Global Investors	$21 billion
Davis Selected Advisers	$20 billion
MetLife Investment Management	$20 billion
CI Segall Bryant & Hamill	$20 billion
TD Epoch Investment Partners	$20 billion
Wilmington Trust	$20 billion
Brandes Investment Partners	$18 billion
Fred Alger Management	$17 billion
Fort Washington Investment Advisors	$17 billion
Lombard Odier	$17 billion
Driehaus Capital Management	$16 billion
Guggenheim Partners	$15 billion
Sumitomo Mitsui DS	$15 billion
Eagle Asset Management	$15 billion
Brown Brothers Harriman	$15 billion
1919 Investment Council	$14 billion
Carmignac Gestion	$13 billion
PineBridge Investments	$12 billion
Magellan Investment Partners	$12 billion
Durable Capital Partners	$11 billion

How to Make a Few *More* Billion Dollars

Liberty Mutual Investments	$10 billion
State Farm Investment Management	$10 billion
Liontrust Asset Management	$10 billion
Mutual of America	$10 billion
New York Life	$10 billion
Odlum Brown	$10 billion
Royce Investment Partners	$10 billion
TCW Investment Management Company	$10 billion
Groupe Bruxelles Lambert	$9 billion
D. F. Dent & Company	$9 billion
Weiss Asset Management	$9 billion
Frontier Capital Management	$9 billion
Gilder Gagnon Howe & Co	$8 billion
Ruane, Cunniff & Goldfarb	$8 billion
Stephens Investment Management	$8 billion
Northwestern Mutual	$7 billion
Australian Foundation Investment Company	$7 billion
Douglas C. Lane	$7 billion
Lyrical Asset Management	$7 billion
Advisors Capital Management	$7 billion
The Glenmede Trust Company	$6 billion
Anchor Capital Advisors	$5 billion
Ingalls & Snyder	$5 billion

Sources and Further Reading

Evolution, Psychology, and Human Behavior

- *Behave: The Biology of Humans at Our Best and Worst* by Robert M. Sapolsky (2017)

- *From Bacteria to Bach and Back: The Evolution of Minds* by Daniel C. Dennett (2017)

- *How to Stubbornly Refuse to Make Yourself Miserable About Anything—Yes, Anything!* by Albert Ellis, Ph.D. (1988)

- *The Adapted Mind: Evolutionary Psychology and the Generation of Culture* by Jerome H. Barkow, Leda Cosmides, and John Tooby (1995)

- *The Descent of Man: An Evolutionary Perspective on Major Depression* by Aaron T. Beck (1992)

- *Up from Dragons: The Evolution of Human Intelligence* by John Skoyles and Dorion Sagan (2002)

Cosmology and Physics

- *Genius: The Life and Science of Richard Feynman* by James Gleick (1992)

- *Relativity: The Special and the General Theory* by Albert Einstein (1916)

- *The Big Bang to Now: A Time Line* by Terry Herman Sissons (2006)

- *The Big Picture: On the Origins of Life, Meaning, and the Universe Itself* by Sean M. Carroll (2016)

- *The First Three Minutes: A Modern View of the Origin of the Universe* by Steven Weinberg (1977)

Futurism and Technology

- *Engines of Creation: The Coming Era of Nanotechnology* by K. Eric Drexler (1986)

- *The Singularity Is Nearer* by Ray Kurzweil (2025)

Business, Strategy, and Management

- *Lean Six Sigma: Combining Six Sigma Quality with Lean Production Speed* by Michael L. George (2002)

- *Lean Thinking: Banish Waste and Create Wealth in Your Corporation* by James P. Womack and Daniel T. Jones (1996)

- *Out of the Crisis* by W. Edwards Deming (1982)

- *The Goal: A Process of Ongoing Improvement* by Eliyahu M. Goldratt (1984)

- *The Toyota Way: 14 Management Principles from the World's Greatest Manufacturer* by Jeffrey K. Liker (2004)

M&A and Corporate Integration

- *After the Merger: The Authoritative Guide for Integration Success* by Price Pritchett (2009)

- *Mastering the Merger: Four Critical Decisions That Make or Break the Deal* by David Harding and Sam Rovit (2004)

- *Mergers, Acquisitions, and Other Restructuring Activities: An Integrated Approach to Process, Tools, Cases, and Solutions* by Donald DePamphilis (2020)

- *The Art of M&A Integration: A Guide to Merging Resources, Processes, and Organizations* by Alexandra Reed Lajoux and Charles Elson (2006)

- *The Synergy Trap* by Mark L. Sirower (1997)

Philosophy, Spirituality, and the Human Condition

- *Centering in Pottery, Poetry, and the Person* by M. C. Richards (1964)

- *Tao Te Ching* by Lao Tzu (2011)

- *The Bhagavad Gita* by Vyasa (2007)

Notes

Chapter 1

1. Lao Tzu, *Tao Te Ching*, English translation (Vintage Books, 2011).

2. Rudolf Otto, *The Idea of the Holy*, 2nd ed. (Oxford University Press, 1958).

3. Tracy Alloway, "What 20 Seconds of Hugging Can Do for You," PsychologyToday.com, January 19, 2022, https://www.psychologytoday.com/us/blog/keep-it-in-mind/202201/what-20-seconds-hugging-can-do-you.

Chapter 2

1. Albert Ellis, *How to Stubbornly Refuse to Make Yourself Miserable About Anything—Yes, Anything!* (Lyle Stuart, 1988).

2. Aaron T. Beck, *Cognitive Therapy and the Emotional Disorders* (International Universities Press, 1976).

3. Aaron T. Beck and Brad A. Alford, *Depression: Causes and Treatment*, 2nd ed. (University of Pennsylvania Press, 2009).

4. Marsha M. Linehan, *Cognitive–Behavioral Treatment of Borderline Personality Disorder* (The Guilford Press, 1993).

5. Linehan, *Cognitive–Behavioral Treatment.*

6. Thích Nhất Hạnh, *Peace Is Every Step: The Path to Mindfulness in Everyday Life* (Random House, 1995).

7. Jon Kabat-Zinn, *Full Catastrophe Living: Using the Wisdom of Your Body and Mind to Face Stress, Pain, and Illness*, rev. ed (Bantam Books, 2013).

Conclusion

1. Ray Kurzweil, *The Singularity Is Near: When Humans Transcend Biology* (Viking Press, 2005).

Index

A

A, B, C players, 119–120, 206–207
Abramovic, Marina, 218
accountability
  backed by change management,
    112–113
  color-coded, 106, 134–135, 146
  corporate culture, imperative to,
    125
acquisitions. *See also* M&A (mergers
    and acquisitions)
  avoiding pitfalls of, 64–65
  B players, keeping, 119
  centralization vs. decentralization,
    113–114
  commitment in, 199
  consultants for, 198
  evaluating, 196–199
  integration and, 94–95
  inventory management,
    revamping, 140–141
  org chart, redesigning, 111–112,
    115–116
  rebranding, 127–128
  talent acquisition, 203–206
  vanity in, 200
aggression, 158, 160
AI. *See* artificial intelligence
alignment, management and
  shareholders, 83–84
analytics, 66–67
anxiety, 33
A players, 119
Apollo Global Management, 81
arrogance, 9
artificial intelligence (AI)
  analyzing industries with, 194
  enabling asymmetric annihilation,
    164–166
  extinction of humanity and,
    162–166
  future life elevated by, 166–172
  impact of, 192
  misuse of, 164–166
  modeled on human thought
    patterns, 158–160

potential uses of, 158–159
silicon-based model powered by, 156–157
wiping out human race, 159–165
The Artist Is Present (Abramovic, Marina), 218
assets under management (AUM), 245–246
asymmetric annihilation, 164–166
attracting top talent, 116, 123
author, experience of, 180
automatic thoughts, 44
automation, 66–67, 193

B

Bandler, Richard, 13–14, 23
Bank of America Merrill Lynch, 86
Beacon Building Products, 98, 103
Beck, Aaron, 30, 43–44
BI. *See* business intelligence
bias, 6, 121, 138, 158, 185
Big Bang, 20–21, 30–31, 233–235
billionaires, living like, 174–177
BlackRock, 86
bliss, meditation and, 12–13
B players, 119
brain
  "feeling the brain" technique, 25–26
  rearranging, 9–10, 182–190
brand integration, 126–128
Breen, Ed, 94
business challenges, as assets, 188
business intelligence (BI), 133–136
  displaying performance data, 97
  salesperson effectiveness, 146

C

capital, raising, 73–92
  debt, 88–89
  endowments and foundations, 84
  family offices, 79–80
  friends and family, 78–79
  hedge funds, 87–88
  investor relations, 90–92
  long-only funds, 85
  passive ETFs, 86–87
  pension plans, 83–84
  private equity, 80–82
  public companies, 75–77
  retail, 86
  sources of equity, 78–89
  sovereign wealth funds, 82
capital allocation, 104, 152
catastrophizing, 33
CBT. *See* cognitive behavioral therapy
centering, 8–10, 45. *See also* recentering
Centering in Pottery, Poetry, and the Person (Richards), 8–9
centralization vs. decentralization, 113–115
change, embracing, 176
change management, 112
Citigroup, 86
Cluster (dynamic art), 187
cognitive behavioral therapy (CBT)
  author using, 186
  automatic thoughts, 44
  centering and, 45
  overview, 43–47
  recentering with, 30

schemas, 43–44
cognitive distortions, 37, 44, 172, 186
Colburn, Dick, 209
collaboration, 137, 214–219
collegiality, 206
color-coded accountability, 106,
    134–135, 146
commitment in acquisitions, 199
communication
    with corporate leaders, 121–122
    with employees, 99–100
    encouraging team members to,
        51–52
    with investors, 90–91
    during meetings, 212–213
    multiple internal channels,
        215–216
    summary from book one, 214–219
    with vendors, 139–140
companies
    creating, author's methodology, 3
    public, benefits of, 75–76
    unrestricted access to, negotiating,
        96
compensation philosophy, 122–124,
    146–147, 149
compensation plans, 122–124,
    207–209
consolidation, choosing industry for,
    57–72
    fragmentation, 64–66
    growth potential, 61–64
    size and scale, 58–61
    tech-backward industries, 66–68
consultants for acquisitions, 198
continual learning, 182

convenience stores industry, 70–71
cooperation, 161
core values, surveying employees
    about, 125–126
corporate culture
    accountability and, 125
    improving, 118
    integrating best aspects of, 124
    respect within, 125
    results-matter, creating, 117
    shifting, 101–102
    spans and layers, 118
    work ethic, 125
corporate integration, 109–128
    brand integration, 126–128
    compensation plans, 122–124
    designing org charts, 110–118
    marrying cultures, 124–126
    sources and further reading,
        261–262
    team building, 119–122
corporate leaders, communication
    with, 121–122
cosmology, 20–21, 30–31, 238–240,
    242–243, 260
Cote, Dave, 94
C players, 119–120
creativity, 4, 16, 18, 20, 25
CRM systems. See customer
    relationship management
    systems
crowdsourcing meeting agenda, 211
Culp, Larry, 94
culture
    of finding value in flaws and
        mistakes, 31–32

integrating in acquisitions,
124–126, 200–201
customer experience
consistent, 114
improving, 68
inconsistent, 113–114
industry, leader in, 60
spans and layers, 118
technology integration and,
143–144
customer feedback loops, 217
customer relationship, 214
customer relationship management
(CRM) systems, 148–149

D

Danaher, 94
data lakehouse, 131, 133, 135
day one, acquisition integration,
95–97
DBT. *See* dialectical behavior therapy
debt, as source of capital, 88–89
decentralization vs. centralization,
113–115
decisions, meditation and, 12
decisiveness, 4–5
demand forecasting, 137–138
dialectical behavior therapy (DBT), 30
emotion mind, 48
middle path, 49
mindfulness and, 50
overview, 47–50
radical acceptance, 47–48
reasonable mind, 48
wise mind, 48–49
dialectical thinking, 184

dilution, 77–78
discipline, 92, 153
in acquisitions, 153
with finances, 88
in focusing on things that move
the needle, 104–105
in getting inventory mix right, 141
in pricing, 146
disruption, 66, 131
disruptive technologies, 192–193
distorted thinking, 45–47
Dixon, Bill, 190, 218
DuPont, 94

E

earnings before interest, taxes,
depreciation, and amortization
(EBITDA)
benefits of, 140
long-only asset management firms
industry, 69–70
procurement and, 138–139
target, 89
e-commerce, 150–152
efficiency
operational, 60
surveying and, 103–104
technology integration and, 136
transportation, 142–143
Einstein, Albert, 7
electric meetings
respectful disagreement, 125
running, 210–214
Ellis, Albert, 3, 30, 35–37
embracing, 48
change, 176

problems as opportunities, 184
emotional balance, 24
emotional regulation, 49, 53
emotions
   anxiety, 33
   bliss, 12–13
   regulating with mindfulness,
      53–54
   reshaping, 9–10
employees
   access to, 96
   A, B, C players, 119–120
   communication with, 99–100
   compensation plans for, 122–123
   connecting with, 101–102
   engagement, 109
   mindfulness toward feelings of, 98
   surveying, 102–104, 125–126
   underutilized, 119
   vetting process, 204–206
endowments
   list of, 251–252
   as source of capital, 84
enterprise resource planning (ERP)
      systems, 131–132, 146
entrepreneurship, 16, 18, 20, 25, 222
equity, compensation plans and, 123
equity capital sources, 78–89, 245–258
   debt, 88–89
   endowments, 84, 251–252
   family offices, 79–80, 246–249
   foundations, 84
   friends and family, 78–79
   hedge funds, 87–88
   long-only funds, 85, 252–258
   passive ETFs, 86–87
   pension plans, 83–84

private equity, 80–82
   retail, 86
   sovereign wealth funds, 82,
      249–251
equity incentives, 208
Erickson, Milton H., 13
ERP. See enterprise resource
      planning system
ETFs. See exchange-traded funds
evolution
   Darwinian adaptability, 155–157
   future of humanity, 156–158
   sources and further reading,
      259–260
   thought experiment, 241–242
evolutionary psychology, 32–34
exchange-traded funds (ETFs),
      68–69

F

family
   as investors, 78–79
family offices, 79-80
   list of, 246–248
   as source of capital, 79–80
fear and anxiety, 6
Federated, 85
feedback loops, 201, 216–217
"feeling the brain" technique, 25–26
Fidelity, 85–86
fiduciary responsibility, 75
field organizations, 120
fight-or-flight response, 33
financial planning and analysis
      (FP&A), 152–153
foundations, as source of capital, 84

fragmentation, industry traits
    checklist, 64–66
free cash flow, 133, 140
friends, as investors, 78–79
future states, 158–174
    AI enabling asymmetric
        annihilation, 164–165
    AI wiping out human race,
        159–165
    beyond utopia, 172–174
    utopia, 166–172

G

gas industry, 70
GE, 94
gedankenexperiments, 182, 187,
    237–243
goal setting, 185
Goldman Sachs, 209, 252
Gottman, John, 24
Gottman, Julie, 24
governance, 80, 112
gratitude conversations, 183
The Great Transformation
    (AI-driven utopia), 166–172
growth potential, industry traits
    checklist, 61–64
GXO Logistics, 219

H

Harik, Mario, 195
hedge funds, as source of capital,
    87–88
Hewson, Marillyn, 94
Hicks, Wayland, 120, 207
Holldobler, Bert, 218

Honeywell, 94
Houston, Dick, 202
Howley, Nick, 94
*How to Stubbornly Refuse to Make
    Yourself Miserable About
    Anything* (Ellis), 36–37
human behavior, 259–260
human condition, 262
human flaws, as maladaptive traits in
    modernity
    aggression, 158, 160
    tribalism, 160–161
humanity
    being wiped out by AI, 159–165
    future evolution of, 156–158
    profit and loss statement of,
        233–235
humanoid robots, 158–159, 171–172
humility, 21, 185
hunger, 205
hypnotherapy, 15–17

I

IC (invested capital), 65
imagination, 23
imperfection mindset, 30–34, 184
incentive structures, 112, 122–123,
    149, 207–209
industries
    analyzing, 191
    convenience stores, 70–71
    ETF, 68–69
    in Europe, 62–64
    fragmentation, 64–66
    gas, 70
    growth, 61–64

long-only asset management
  firms, 69–70
modernizing, 67–68
in North America, 62–64
oil, 70
organic growth in, 61–62
scalability of, 59–60
size of, 58–61
tech backwards, 66–68
total addressable market, 58–61
industry traits checklist, 57–72
fragmentation, 64–66
growth potential, 61–64
size and scale, 58–61
tech-backward industries, 66–68
inner control, 8–10
innovation, 222, 225
  to accelerate growth, 194
  acceleration of, 157
  developing agenda for, 192
  directing toward outcomes that
    uplift humanity, 176
  mass disasters enabled by, 165
  at Philipp Brothers, 188
  at United Rentals, 221
  at XPO, 196
integration, 93–107, 155–156
  acquisitions and, 94–95, 200–201
  AI, 136
  of corporate culture, 124
  day one, 95–97
  doubling profit and, goal of, 128
  early integration, 104–107
  employee surveys and, 102–104
  ERP systems, 131–132
  methodical transformation, 107

micromanaging and, 105
POS systems, 132–133
technology integration, 132
town halls, 97–102
tracking, 105–107
integrity, 205–206
intelligence, 204–205
inventory management
  e-commerce, 151
  integrating technology into,
    140–141
  predictive, 133
  WMS, 141
Invesco, 85
invested capital (IC), 65
investor relations, 90–92
investors
  Apollo Global Management, 81
  Bank of America Merrill Lynch, 86
  BlackRock, 86–87
  Citigroup, 86
  communication with, 90–91, 217
  endowments, 84
  family and friends as, 78–79
  family offices, 79–80
  Federated, 85
  Fidelity, 85–86
  foundations, 84
  hedge funds, 87
  Invesco, 85
  Janus Henderson, 85
  JPMorgan Chase, 86
  long-only asset management
    firms, 85
  Morgan Stanley, 86
  Orbis, 85

passive ETFs, 86–87
pension plans, 83
private equity funds, 80–81
retail, 86
sovereign wealth funds, 82–83
State Street, 86–87
United Rentals, 81
Vanguard, 86–87
Wells Fargo, 86
irrational beliefs, 38–42

J

Janus Henderson, 85
Jesselson, Ludwig, 188
JPMorgan Chase, 86
judgment, suspending, 185

K

Kabat-Zinn, Jon, 52–53
key performance indicators (KPIs), 97, 133–134
Kurzweil, Ray, 157, 172, 193

L

Large, Sad Sphere sculpture, 186
leadership, 6
  by author, 180–181
  balanced mindset and, 8
  cash utilization by leadership teams, 74
  centralization and, 113
  importance of, 120
  leadership talent, 3
  org charts and, 112

Lean Six Sigma, 9–10
learning, continual, 182
Linehan, Marsha, 30, 47–49
listening, 216
  with feedback loops, 99, 103–104
  intently, 48
Lockheed Martin, 94
logistics. *See* transportation and logistics
long-only asset management firms, 252–258
long-only funds
  asset management firms industry, 69–70
  list of, 252–258
  as source of capital, 85
love and meditation, 20–22
love vibes, 24, 183

M

M&A (mergers and acquisitions)
  bingo quadrant, 188
  sources and further reading, 261–262
  summary from book one, 196–203
management
  alignment between shareholders and, 83–84
  sources and further reading, 261
marketing, 76, 86
MBSR (mindfulness-based stress reduction), 53
meditation, 7–27, 187
  author's path, 12 14
  Big Bang and, 21
  bliss and, 12–13

centering, 8–10
cosmology and, 21
decisions and, 12
"feeling the brain" technique,
25–26
hypnotherapy, 15–17
mental synthesis, 10–11
mind–hand connection exercise,
17–18
mixing with schools of thought,
13–14
morning routine, 14–19
movie screen, 22–24
multiverse visualization
techniques, 15–16
numinous experiences, 19–20
playing with time, space, and love,
20–22
pranayama breathing exercise,
18–19
Qigong techniques, 14–15
toward own center, 26–27
universe visualization techniques,
15–16
visualization techniques, 15–16,
20–21
meetings
electric, 125, 210–214
KPI dashboard data, 134–135
running electric, 210–214
mental synthesis, 10–11
mergers and acquisitions. *See* M&A
micromanaging, 105
middle path, 49
mindfulness, 52–55
benefits of, 53
DBT and, 50
Jon Kabat-Zinn, 53

meditation and, 22–23
of others, 54, 98
regulating emotions with, 53–54
Thích Nhất Hạnh, 14, 52–53
mindfulness-based stress reduction
(MBSR), 53
mind–hand connection exercise,
17–18
mindset
arrogance, 9
clear and balanced, 8
imperfect, 31–32
modern breakthrough technologies,
157–158, 166
Morgan Stanley, 86
morning routine, 14–19
movie screen meditation, 22–24
multiple arbitrage, 65
multiverse visualization techniques,
15–16, 240, 243

N

Nhất Hạnh, Thích, 14, 52–53
natural selection vs. unnatural, 157
negative thoughts, 183–184
negotiating deals, 196
numinous experiences, 19–20

O

"obscene profits," 197–198
oil industry, 70
on-time and in-full (OTIF)
performance, 134
operating reviews, 212
operational integration, 201
optimism, 64, 93, 221

Orbis, 85
organic growth, 61–62
organizational culture, 124–126
org chart design, 110–118
    centralization vs. decentralization,
        113–115
    growth and change, 115–117
    spans and layers, 117–118
OTIF (on-time and in-full)
    performance, 134
Otterness, Tom, 186
Otto, Rudolf, 19–20

P

passive ETFs, 86–87
pensions, 83–84,
    list of, 249–251
perceptions, reshaping, 9–10
perfectionism
    evolution and, 33–34
    as irrational belief, 39
    REBT and, 36–37
performance-based compensation,
    146–147, 149
philosophy, 262
physics, 260
playing with time, space, and love,
    20–22
point-of-sale (POS) systems,
    132–133
positive psychology, 50–52
post-human future, 166–174
pranayama breathing exercise, 18–19
pricing
    centralization vs. decentralization,
        114–115
    elasticity, 145–146
    optimization of, 145–147

private equity, 80–82
private investments in public equity
    (PIPEs), 81, 87
problems, embracing as
    opportunities, 184
procurement, 138–140
    centralized/decentralized, 113–
        114, 139
    costs of, 60
productivity, 60, 141
promises during negotiations, 200
psychological reframing, 49–50
psychology, 259–260
public companies, 75–77
public equity markets, 180

Q

Qigong techniques, 14–15
QXO
    analyzing trends in industries, 59
    industry traits checklist and, 57
    OTIF performance, 134
    survey of core values, 125–126

R

radical acceptance, 47–48, 184–185,
    189
raising capital. *See* capital, raising
raising the qi, 15
Rales, Steven, 94
rational beliefs, 39–42
rational emotive behavior therapy
    (REBT), 30, 34–43
rearranging brain, 9–10
reasonable mind, 48
rebranding, 127–128
recentering, 29–55. *See also* centering

Cognitive Behavioral Therapy
(CBT), 43–47
Dialectical Behavior Therapy
(DBT), 47–50
evolutionary psychology, 32–34
imperfection mindset, 30–32
mindfulness, 52–55
positive psychology, 50–52
Rational Emotive Behavior
Therapy (REBT), 34–43
reframing thinking, 45–47
resilience, 27, 50, 184, 187
respect, 40
for employees, 102, 201
for sellers, 200
when disagreeing, 125, 210–213
respectful disagreement, 125
results-matter culture, 117
retail, as source of capital, 86
return on invested capital (ROIC), 65
return-to-center. *See* recentering
Richards, M. C., 8–9
risk management
acceptable risk, 196–197
of family offices, 79
of hedge funds, 88
irrational belief, 42
of pension plans, 83–84
transportation and logistics,
142–143
ROIC. *See* return on invested capital
Rossi, Ernie, 17, 25
routine, morning, 14–19
runners-up industries, 68–72
RXO, 136, 176, 181, 196, 208

S

sales commission structure, 149
sales force effectiveness, 147–150
scalability, 59–60, 144
Schatz, Lincoln, 187
schemas, 43–45
schools of thought, mixing
meditation with, 13–14
self-criticism, 36
Seligman, Martin, 30, 50, 185–186
shareholder alignment, 83–84
shareholder value
attracting top talent, 116, 122
creating, 4, 69, 153
customer experience and, 153
industry traits checklist, 58
overpaying for acquisition, 66
share prices, returns on, 6
singularity, 172–174, 234
The Singularity Is Near (Kurzweil,
R.), 193–194
size and scale, 58–61, 197
smart money, 73
sources and further reading, 259–262
business, strategy, and
management, 261
cosmology and physics, 260
evolution, psychology, and human
behavior, 259–260
futurism and technology, 260
M&A and corporate integration,
261–262
philosophy, spirituality, and
human condition, 262
sovereign wealth funds
as source of capital, 82–83
list of, 248–249

space and meditation, 20–22
spans and layers, 117–118
speed, 4–5, 199
spirituality, 262
State Street, 86–87
stinkin' thinkin', 36–37
stocks, 77–78, 123
strategy, 261
succession planning, 212
The Superorganism (Holldobler and Wilson), 218
superorganisms, 161, 215
surveying, 125–126
synergies, 93
systems integration, 130–137

T

talent acquisition, 203–206
talent evaluation system, 206–207
TAM (total addressable market), 58–61
Tao Te Ching (Tzu), 9
teams
    building, 119–122, 203–209
    encouraging communication between, 51–52
tech-backward industries, 66–68
technology, 225–232
    forecasting developments in, 193
    research and investing in, 191–192
    sources and further reading, 260
technology integration, 129–153
    BI, 133–136
    demand forecasting, 137–138
    e-commerce, 150 152

financial planning and analysis, 152–153
humanity and, 167–172
inventory management, 140–141
predictive analytics, 137–138
pricing KPI, 146
pricing optimization, 145–147
procurement, 138–140
sales force effectiveness, 147–150
systems integration, 130–137
tactical use of, 150
TMS, 142
transportation and logistics, 141–144
utopian society, 172–177
WMS, 141
techno sapiens, 235
Thay. *See* Nhất Hạnh, Thích
thinking big from day one, 4
thinking differently, 182
thought experiments as creative catalysts, 237–243
thought patterns
    AI modeled on, 159–160
    automatic, 44
    distorted, 45–47
    reframing, 45–47
    reshaping, 9–10
time and meditation, 20–22
TM (transcendental meditation), 12–13
TMS (transportation management system), 142
tools developed by humans, 225–232
total addressable market (TAM), 58–61

total shareholder return (TSR), 123
town halls
  crowdsourcing principles in, 213
  dynamic, 99
  integration playbook, 97–102
tracker systems, 106, 134–135, 146
TransDigm, 94
transportation and logistics, 141–144, 193
transportation management system (TMS), 142
trends, 190–196
tribalism, 160–161
TSR (total shareholder return), 123
Tzu, Lao, 9

U

ultimate opportunity, 155–174
  AI enabling asymmetric annihilation, 164–165
  AI wiping out human race, 159–165
  beyond utopia, 172–174
  living like billionaires, 174–177
  new paradigm, 156–158
  potential future states, 158–174
  utopia, 166–172
unified team culture, 215
United Rentals, 6, 81
  achievements of, 221
  founding of, 181
  innovation in, 195
United Waste Systems
  consolidation of, 202
  founding of, 181

innovation in, 195
universe visualization techniques, 15–16
university endowments, 222, 251–252
unnatural selection
  vs. natural selection, 157
  time line, 225–232
utopia
  beyond, 172–174
  Great Transformation, 167–172
  overview, 166–167

V

valuation multiples, 76, 88
Vanguard, 86–87
vanity in acquisitions, 200
visualization techniques, 15–16, 20–21, 237–243

W

warehouse management system (WMS), 141
warehouses, optimizing, 67–68
waste of time/waste of money (WOT-WOM), 101
wealth
  obsolescence of, in utopian economy, 191
  pursuit of, 190
Wells Fargo, 86
Wilson, E.O., 218
wise mind, 48–49
work ethic, 125

X

XPO, 57
  achievements of, 221
  digital marketplace, 136
  founding of, 181
  innovation in, 195–196
  integrating acquisitions, 203
  proactive communication
    example, 219
  stock, 6
  talent acquisition for, 209
  technology, tactical use of, 150
  transportation efficiency, 142–143
  weeding out brands, 127

Y

yoga, 14

About the Author

BRAD JACOBS is an American entrepreneur and a career CEO with a unique track record as a Wall Street moneymaker. He has founded and led eight companies, including six publicly traded, multibillion-dollar corporations: United Waste Systems, United Rentals, XPO and its spin-offs RXO and GXO Logistics, and now QXO, one of the world's largest building products distributors. Over the course of his career, he has completed approximately 500 M&A transactions, raised over $50 Billion of debt and equity capital, and created tens of billions of dollars in shareholder value.

Jacobs grew XPO into a top 10 global logistics provider and the seventh-best-performing stock of the last decade in the Fortune 500. XPO's stock became a "50-bagger"—initial investors in 2011 made more than 50 times their money. United Rentals was the sixth-best-performing stock during the same period and is now more than a "200-bagger." United Waste's stock outperformed the S&P 500 by 5.6 times over five years, from the time Jacobs took the company public to when it was sold in 1997.

Jacobs is chairman and CEO of QXO and executive chairman of XPO.